Real-Life
CRIMES
...and how they were solved

Forensic Mysteries

CHANCELLOR
PRESS

First published in Great Britain in 1994 by Chancellor Press
an imprint of Reed Consumer Books Limited
Michelin House
81 Fulham Road
London SW3 6RB
and Auckland, Melbourne, Singapore and Toronto

by arrangement with Eaglemoss Publications Ltd

The material in this book first appeared in partwork form

ISBN 1 85152 489 4

A CIP catalogue record for this book is available at the British Library

Printed and bound in China
Produced by Mandarin Offset

Picture acknowledgements
Front cover: *(main)* Topham Picture source; *(left)* Jerry Young; *(centre)* Science Photo Library; *(right)* Aerospace Publishing. **5:** Midsummer Books/Prof. Bernard Knight/Prof. Bernard Knight. **6:** South Wales Constabulary/Jerry Young. **7:** Oxford Scientific/Oxford Scientific/Oxford Scientific. **8:** Jerry Young. **9:** Jerry Young/Jerry Young/Topham Picture Source. **10:** South Wales Constabulary/Jerrry Young. **11:** South Wales Constabulary/Midsummer Books. **12-13:** Metro Dade Medical Examiners Office, Miami. **13:** Miami Herald. **14:** Miami Herald/Miami Herald/Metro Dade/Metro Dade. **15:** Metro Dade/Miami Herald/Metro Dade/Metro Dade. **16-17:** Metro Dade. **18:** Metro Dade/AP/Wideworld Photos/Miami Herald. **19:** News Team International. **20:** News Team International/Science Photo Library. **21:** News Team International. **22:** Birmingham Post & Mail/News Team International/News Team International. **23:** Science Photo Library/Science Photo Library/Birmingham Post & Mail. **24:** Miami Herald/Metro Dade Medical Examiners Office, Miami. **25:** Metro Dade Medical Examiners Office, Miami. **26:** Metro Dade Medical Examiners Office, Miami. **27:** Miami Herald/Miami Herald/Metro Dade Medical Examiners Office, Miami. **28:** Topham Picture Source/Topham Picture Source. **29:** Topham Picture Source/Topham Picture Source. **30:** Aerospace Publishing/Topham Picture Source/Aerospace Publishing. **31:** Syndication International. **32:** Topham Picture Source/Topham Picture Source/Syndication International. **33:** Syndication International/Topham Picture Source. **34-37:** Topham Picture Source. **38.** Nottingham Evening Post – T. Bailey Forman Ltd/Nottinghamshire Constabulary. **39-42:** Nottinghamshire Constabulary/Nottinghamshire Constabulary/University of Sheffield/Nottinghamshire Constabulary/Nottinghamshire Constabulary/Nottingham Evening Post. **43:** University of Sheffield (four). **44:** Frank Spooner//David C. Isby. **45:** Frank Spooner/AP/Wideworld Photos/Frank Spooner/Frank Spooner. **46:** AP/Wideworld Photos. **47:** Frank Spooner/Frank Spooner. **48:** Rex Features/Rex Features. **50:** John Frost/Rex Features/Rex Features. **51:** Midsummer. **52:** Express Newspapers/Press Association. **53:** Rex Features/Rex Features. **54:** Robert Harding/Robert Harding. **55:** Metro Dade Medical Examiners Office, Miami/Miami Herald/AP/Wideworld Photos/Metro Dade/Metro Dade. **57:** Miami Herald/AP/Wideworld Photos/Metro Dade/Metro Dade. **58-63:** Metro Dade Medical Examiners Office, Miami. **63:** Metro Dade Medical Examiners Office, Miami/Miami Herald. **64:** Dragon News & Picture Agency/Dragon News & Picture Agency/Dragon News & Picture Agency. **65:** Dragon News & Picture Agency/Dragon News & Picture Agency/Dragon News & Picture Agency/Topham Picture Source/John Frost. **66:** John Frost/Dragon News & Picture Agency/Dragon News & Picture Agency. **67:** John Frost. **68:** Dragon News & Picture Agency/Dragon News & Picture Agency. **69:** Syndication International/The Reporter Series Ltd./Spenborough Guardian. **70:** Syndication International. **71:** Spenborough Guardian/Syndication International. **72:** Popperfoto/The Reporter Series Ltd./Spenborough Guardian. **74:** Yorkshire Evening Post. **75:** Syndication International/Ross Parry Picture Agency/Yorkshire Evening Post – British Library, Colindale. **76:** Cardiff Royal Infirmary. **77:** South Wales Echo/Cardiff Royal Infirmary. **78:** Cardiff Royal Infirmary. **79:** Cardiff Royal Infirmary/Illustrated London News. **80:** Cardiff Royal Infirmary/Richard Whittington – Egan/Cardiff Royal Infirmary.

CONTENTS

Top inset: Fitzhamon Embankment is a short street running down the banks of the River Taff in Cardiff. Workmen renovating a house in the street made the gruesome discovery of the body in the carpet.

Above and left: Night was falling when the skeleton was found. It had been buried in a rear garden, wrapped in a black plastic bin liner and a carpet, before being tied with electrical flex. Pathologists and scene-of-crime officers made a careful examination of the body and of the garden from which the remains were unearthed.

The Skeleton in the CARPET

Nobody knew who she was or how long her body had been buried. But the investigators had a wide range of forensic techniques to help them solve the mystery.

The pathetic remains of her body were unearthed from their makeshift grave on 7 December 1989. Building workers were deepening a trench in the rear garden of No. 29 Fitzhamon Embankment in Cardiff when a spade struck something soft, about 18 inches down.

They uncovered a rolled-up carpet, tied with electrical flex. Inside, to their horror, was a skeleton, still dressed in socks, brassiere and panties, together with the almost rotted remains of a sweatshirt and trousers.

Within this rough and ready shroud were the clues that would launch police and forensic scientists on a remarkable voyage of discovery. It would not only identify the victim, but, more than nine years after the crime, lead to the trial and conviction of two ruthless killers.

Police at scene

The police were called immediately, and arrived at Fitzhamon Embankment as darkness fell. Detective Chief Super-

intendent John Williams, head of South Wales CID, took charge of the case. The scene was cordoned off, and forensic teams went to work.

The pathologist on the case was Professor Bernard Knight, Professor of Forensic Pathology at the University of Wales and one of Britain's leading experts in forensic medicine. After a preliminary examination on site, Professor Knight had the remains transported to Cardiff Royal Infirmary for a more thorough investigation.

The hands and body had been tied with

5

Mystery

When did she buy these clothes?

The victim's clothes were analysed at the Chepstow laboratory of the Home Office's Forensic Science Service. Most were standard chain-store items, including 'Karman Ghia' slacks and a 'Shadowline' bra. Enquiries to manufacturers and stores in the area revealed that all of the items would have been on sale in South Wales in the early 1980s. The victim had also been wearing a distinctive grey sweatshirt. Made in America by Levi-Strauss specifically for the British market, that pattern had been manufactured in December 1980. Thus the body could not have been buried before early 1981.

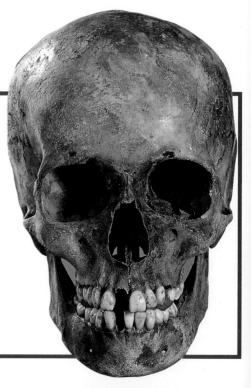

Above: Some of the clothes worn by the victim – those including man-made fibres or coloured with artificial dyes – survived intact. Both socks were present when the body was found.

Inset: A pair of simple golden earstuds, discovered when the carpet containing the body was unrolled for the post-mortem examination, were the only personal items found in the grave.

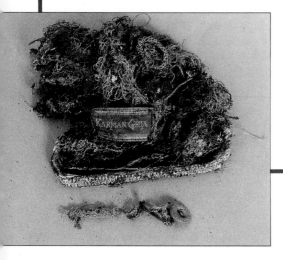

Left: Although the victim's cotton trousers had been almost completely eaten away, a button and the designer's label survived, enabling the forensic scientists to identify the brand.

black electric cable, and the upper part of the body had been covered in a black plastic bin liner. There was a full head of blonde hair, but very little tissue remained attached to the skeleton. Nevertheless, by 11 p.m. the professor and his team had come to certain conclusions.

They had determined that the victim was a blonde-haired Caucasian girl, either European or Indo-European, probably in her late teens or early 20s. The body was almost completely skeletalised, which in the open air can occur in months, but when buried would be unlikely to take less than two years. This dated the crime to before 1987.

There were no immediate signs of the cause of death, but the circumstances in which the body had been clandestinely concealed made it almost certain that there had been foul play.

Dental investigation

Further investigation by Professor Knight and by University of Wales dental expert Dr David Whittaker was to refine the assessment, estimating the victim's height to have been about five feet two or three inches, and her age at death to have been between 14 and 16 years. Whittaker's techniques of X-ray analysis of teeth and

their roots have proved very accurate in estimating the age of adolescents, and he was later able to narrow her age down still further to about 15½ years old.

While the examination of the body continued, the clothes were sent for analysis at the Chepstow laboratory of the Home Office's Forensic Science Service. They determined that the victim had been dressed in a 'Shadowline' bra, a pair of chain-store knickers, a pair of pink patterned socks, a Levi-Strauss sweatshirt and a pair of trousers. The trousers had

almost completely rotted away, but their 'Karman Ghia' designer label was still visible. A pair of small golden earstuds had been found in the folds of the carpet.

A real-life murder investigation is rarely the non-stop drama that is portrayed on television. Most operations are tediously routine, and so it proved for the team assigned to trace the origin of the clothes. But within a month they had made some progress.

It was established that all of the articles

How old was she?

The first step in a murder investigation is to establish the sex and age of the victim. In the Cardiff case, the skeleton was complete, which meant that it was fairly easy to see that the victim was female. Lack of tooth wear indicated a fairly young person, in her teens or early twenties. X-rays showed teeth still developing, from which Dr David Whittaker was able to estimate that the victim was 15½ years old.

The victim's skull gave many clues to her identity, and ultimately provided proof of who she was.

would have been on sale in Cardiff during the early years of the 1980s. Moreover, the grey sweatshirt had been made in America by Levi-Strauss specifically for the British market. That pattern of shirt had been manufactured in December 1980; thus the body could not have been buried earlier than 1981.

Now Detective Chief Superintendent Williams had some details with which to work. However, the 'early 1980s' had swallowed up more than its share of missing persons, and establishing the identity of one girl among the many was going to be a problem.

'Bugs and beetles' man

John Williams was determined to leave no avenue unexplored in his search for the victim's identity. For a start, if he was to get a result he would have to tighten up the estimate of the time of death.

Enter Zakaria Erzinclioglu of Cambridge University, known as 'Doctor Zak' to his police colleagues. Doctor Zak is the 'bugs and beetles' man; more formally he is Britain's only forensic entomologist.

He examines the live and dead insect life associated with human remains when they are found, as well as in the surrounding soil. From that information he could estimate that the body had been in the ground for at least five years, which placed the date of the crime before 1984.

As an incidental piece of information, Dr Zak told the police that, from the evidence of eggs laid by bluebottles, the body had not been buried until at least a day after death.

Anthropologists from the Natural History Museum in London were the next specialists to be consulted, specifically about the victim's skull. Comparing it with known skulls in their records, they declared that from the shape the victim had been a white European, but the shape and size of the teeth indicated that she had

Timetable of the coffin flies

Doctor Zakaria Erzinclioglu examines the insect life on and around buried bodies. By comparing them with the known life-cycles and feeding habits of the insects, he can give a remarkably accurate estimate of the time the body has been in place.

The unknown girl's grave in Cardiff yielded a quantity of dried pupal cases left behind after the emergence of Phorid flies – popularly known as 'coffin flies'. These burrow down into the soil, where they feed on dead bodies.

Based on a calculation of the time it would have taken the flies to eat their way through the soft tissues of the body, 'Little Miss Nobody' would have had to have been in the ground for at least three years.

Once the coffin flies had exposed the bones, they had been replaced by a well-established colony of several generations of woodlice, attracted by the fungus growing on the de-fleshed skeleton.

'Doctor Zak' estimated that the colony would have needed two years to establish itself, which, when added to the three years needed for the coffin flies to do their work, meant that the body had been buried for at least five years. This placed the time of death some time before 1984.

STAGE 2:

'Coffin flies' had burrowed through the soil to lay their eggs in the body, taking three years to strip the corpse of flesh.

STAGE 3:

Once the coffin flies had exposed the bones, fungus grew and woodlice established a colony, grazing on the fungus-coated remains.

STAGE 1:

The presence of blowfly maggots and pupae showed that the body had not been buried immediately.

probably been at least partly of foreign parentage.

Meanwhile, the relentless progress of 'routine enquiries' had begun to locate former residents of 27 and 29 Fitzhamon Embankment. At about the time the victim

would have disappeared, the knocked-together pair of houses had been let out as single rooms or small flats. Police estimated that more than 700 people had lived there in the 1980s, so tracing occupants after so many years was a time-consuming assignment.

Carpet identified

Nevertheless, one notable success was that the six-feet by five-feet section of carpet in which the body had been buried was

When did she die?

Establishing the time of death was vital to discovering who the victim was. By correlating the evidence of the age of the clothing and the insect activity on the body, forensic investigators were able to reduce from nine to 3½ years the period during which death had taken place.

1980	1981	1982	1983	1984	1985	1986	1987	1988	1989
Latest possible date of burial from pathological evidence. →→→									
	←←← Earliest possible date of burial from evidence of clothing.								
Latest possible date of burial from insect evidence. →→→									
←←← Period in which the body must have been buried. →→→									

Facing the unknown

Richard Neave of the University of Manchester was asked to reconstruct the dead girl's face. "I'm only called in when the remains are beyond recognition," he comments. "Hopefully, the police are going to give me a certain amount of information, perhaps gained from the forensic pathologist on the case. The more information I can get the better. Ideally, I need to know the age, sex, ethnic group, and stature. Evidence of hair type and length will also be useful."

"Sometimes, there is very little information available. With the girl from Cardiff, all I had was the skull, with some indication of hair length. In other cases, the body might have been in a ditch for weeks. In such conditions, there is rarely much to work with. Bodies in the open lose their flesh very fast. Birds will pick out the eyes, foxes will take off the nose, rats will eat anything."

"However, what I'm most likely to get is a policeman leaving me with a festering heap in a plastic bag, saying 'We think it's a male between 40 and 60, but we're still waiting for the pathologist's report'. I'll do what I have to do, but in the absence of any further information, I have to use my own experience."

Taking a cast of the head as soon as it is delivered preserves any features that survive. The skull is then defleshed, all the rotting matter being taken along with any insects. The lower jaw is attached to the clean skull, and dummy eyeballs are inserted. Another mould is made, from which a plaster cast of the skull is taken.

Richard Neave, senior medical artist at the University of Manchester, is Britain's leading expert in facial reconstruction. He developed his skills as an aid to archaeologists working on ancient mummies. However, reconstruction is also an effective forensic technique, and he has been called in to help on a number of baffling cases.

identified by a former tenant, and the supplier's fitter was found, who confirmed that just such an offcut was left over at the time the basement flat was carpeted.

But what Detective Chief Superintendent Williams wanted most was a face; the features that had once graced the anonymous skull of 'Little Miss Nobody'.

One of John Williams' sergeants recalled seeing a television programme in which artist Richard Neave from the University of Manchester Medical School had reconstructed the face of an archaeological find using only the skull as reference. He suggested that the technique might be used here.

Facial reconstruction is not new; it was pioneered by Mikhail Gerasimov in Moscow in the 1920s.

The process is disarmingly simple. The 'equipment' required consists of clay, modelling tools, and cocktail sticks cut into pegs. However, it also requires the hand and eye of the artist and the specialised knowledge of the anatomist.

Neave agreed to help, and the unknown victim's skull was sent north by car. Over two days at the end of December 1989 he worked in his studio to recreate the face of the nameless teenager. Once completed,

the reconstruction was photographed from several angles.

It was characteristic of the professional way in which John Williams was conducting his enquiry that he had a contingency plan in case Neave had difficulty with his reconstruction.

A possible name

The skull was sent to Dr Peter Vanezis, then a senior lecturer in forensic medicine at the London Hospital. Vanezis was involved in recent experiments using high technology to 'fill out' the features of a skull. He uses laser, video cameras and computers where Richard Neave uses clay, but the aim is similar.

As it happened, the computer reconstruction was not needed. At the beginning of the New Year, photographs of the clay portrait had been distributed to the press and television, and official posters carrying the pictures and a request for help from the public were put on display. It is a tribute to Richard Neave's skills that the police had only a couple of days to wait before they had a possible name to fit their face.

A Cardiff social worker thought that 'Little Miss Nobody' could be a former

client, a 15-year-old who had absconded eight years earlier from the children's home and assessment centre in which she had been placed. Her name was Karen Price.

She was certainly of the right age, and had disappeared at the right time. But the absolute identification necessary for a coroner's inquest was lacking. However, with a name, police could try to find relevant dental records.

Dental records found

After making personal visits to all the dentists and dental care clinics in the Cardiff area, the investigators were rewarded when Karen Price's dental chart was located. Doctor Whittaker was confident that it matched the skull that had been found.

Final confirmation of Karen Price's identity was established through use of a new technique that has revolutionised the positive identification of human beings – the comparison of DNA profiles, or 'genetic fingerprinting'. DNA extracted from the Cardiff bones was compared with DNA drawn from blood samples given by Karen's parents. They left no doubt that the remains uncovered at Fitzhamon Embankment were those of Karen Price.

How she met her death, and at whose hands, were harder questions to answer.

Over the years, BBC Television's *Crimewatch UK* programme has become something of a national institution. The programme offers a monthly dossier of crime reconstructions and requests made

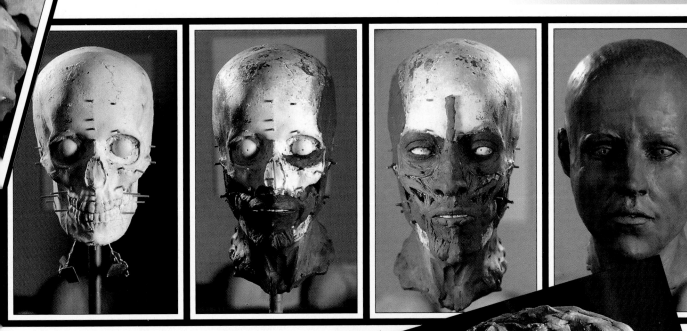

Richard Neave began work at 10 a.m. on 18 December. Pegs representing standard depths of flesh were inserted at various points, and clay representing the muscle groups of the mouth was then laid down. Neave could then begin fitting the sheets of clay representing the skin and the nose was in place by 4 p.m. The next morning he worked on completing the face, with the final touch being the addition of the hair (right).

by the police for 'help with their inquiries'. It was just the kind of help that might provide Detective Chief Superintendant Williams with the last piece of his already remarkable jig-saw puzzle. The vital clue that would prevent Karen Price becoming just another "cause of death unknown" entry in the coroner's records.

Crimewatch link

One evening a young man named Meic Corcoran, his wife and her friend, and Meic's friend Idris Ali were keeping their regular date with *Crimewatch*: it happened

Below: Once the portrait of the unknown was finished, Detective Chief Superintendent John Williams held a press conference, and the image of the unknown girl then appeared in newspapers and on television.

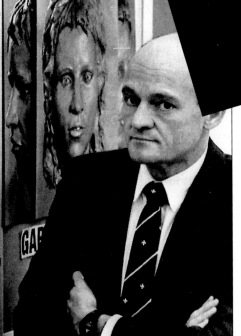

GARDEN BODY A GIRL OF ABOUT 16

to be the edition on which John Williams was appealing for help. Suddenly Idris broke their spellbound silence: "I knew her . . . I used to go around with her!"

Vital information

Although he was reluctant at first to come forward with his information, Ali was finally persuaded by his friends that it was his duty to help; after all, what was it the TV presenter had said: "If you were a friend of Karen's then, be a friend to her now." And Idris *had* been a friend. Within hours he was being interviewed by a

9

Karen identified

Left: Whatever the actual likeness of the Richard Neave clay model, it triggered the memory of a viewer who saw the Crimewatch programme.

The purpose of the reconstruction carried out by Richard Neave was not to create an absolutely faithful likeness of the unknown girl, but to produce something close enough to jog some memories. Sure enough, within days of the reconstruction being publicised a number of possible identifications were received. Most were tracked down and eliminated from the enquiry, but one seemed more promising. A social worker suggested that it looked a bit like a runaway, Karen Price, who had not been seen since 1981.

detective, and said that he had first met Karen 12 years previously when they were at school together. He claimed he had last seen her in July 1981, with a group of friends in a Cardiff park.

As a result of Idris Ali's information, others of Karen's friends and acquaintances were traced, and slowly the picture of her unhappy lifestyle as a runaway began to emerge. A significant part of the group's social activities appeared to centre on a bar in Caroline Street, Cardiff, where another, older acquaintance, Alan Charlton, was employed as a doorman. Coincidentally, the police learned, Alan Charlton was at that time living in the basement flat at 27-29 Fitzhamon Embankment.

With a little more persuasion over the course of a number of interviews, Idris Ali confided to his questioners that while his pal Charlton was making a living out of his muscles he, Ali, was earning a dishonest living pimping for Karen Price and one of her friends; and that one of his customers was Alan Charlton. There was worse to come.

Pornographic photographs

On a day which was probably late in July 1981, Charlton invited Karen, her friend and Idris Ali back to his basement flat. Here, according to Karen's friend Ali, Charlton insisted the girls take off their

clothes and pose for some pornographic photographs. When they indignantly refused, and Karen became abusive, Charlton "went berserk" and attacked her with fists and feet, and eventually strangled her.

In a later statement Ali confessed his part in the events, though Charlton, taken into custody and questioned, denied any part in the killing of Karen Price; indeed, he denied even knowing Karen. For that matter he denied knowing Idris Ali as well.

But if Alan Charlton was saying nothing, Idris Ali was doing enough talking for both of them. He was telling detectives how he helped Alan dig a large hole at the end of the garden at Fitzhamon Embankment! Meanwhile another friend of Karen's was

10

The lost life of Karen Price

Karen Price had been a happy child, who had become a seriously disturbed teenager. Falling into bad company, she was murdered before her life was fairly under way.

Karen Price was born in Cardiff on 4 September 1965, to Anita and Michael Price. Although both natives of Cardiff, Karen's parents could claim between them such widely varying ancestry as Cypriot, Spanish, American, and Welsh.

They were married in 1959, but by 1971 the relationship had deteriorated, and a dark shadow had been cast over Karen's young life that was rarely to lift until her death.

After her parents split up Karen lived with her father, but began to show signs of disturbed behaviour. In 1975 a social order was made, taking Karen into care: she was just 10 years old. She spent the next five years of her life living in a Salvation Army home and attending a special school for disturbed children.

In the early May of 1981, Karen was moved to a children's home and assessment centre at Pontypridd, from which she absconded and was brought back several times before her final disappearance on 2 July 1981. At that point, as far as the authorities were concerned, the Karen Price story came to an abrupt end.

Later it was revealed that Karen had moved back to Cardiff, where in the last month of her life she had drifted into prostitution. It was probably at the end of July or the beginning of August that she was killed and buried in the back garden of 29 Fitzhamon Embankment.

busy picking Charlton out of a police line-up as the man she had seen with Karen. As for his friendship with Ali, that too was attested by independent witnesses who had seen them together frequently in the bar where Charlton was a bouncer.

On 25 February 1990, Alan Charlton and Idris Ali were jointly charged with the murder of Karen Price "on some date between 1 July 1981 and 1 May 1982". Karen's girlfriend, who had witnessed the crime and been frightened into silence ever since, became the chief witness for the Crown.

"Overwhelming evidence"

By comparison with the extraordinary complexity of the investigation and the dramatic exposure of the killers, the trial of Charlton and Ali at Cardiff Crown Court during January and February 1991 was something of an anti-climax. By what Mr Justice Rose, the presiding judge, described as "overwhelming evidence", both defendants were convicted – Idris Ali, who had been just 16 years old at the time of Karen's murder, was ordered to be detained during Her Majesty's pleasure. Charlton, who had been 21, was sentenced to life imprisonment – the judge identifying him as "playing the greater part".

The tragic death of Karen Price nine years earlier had, thanks to the tenacity of John Williams and his squad, and with no little help from science and the media, been avenged. □

Right: Once the police knew who it was they were looking for, they heard from people who remembered Karen Price being in Cardiff in the summer of 1981. One of the last times she was seen was in Astey's cafe, by Cardiff's rail and bus stations.

Below: Just across the River Taff from the Welsh national rugby stadium, Fitzhamon Embankment was a downmarket area in the early 1980s. It was in a basement flat here that Karen Price had the life choked out of her.

TRIPLE MURDER

at the World of Health

Above: The first evidence of the massacre at the World of Health Spa was when the body of owner John Mitchell, lying sprawled inside the entrance, was found by his father.

The World of Health Spa was the kind of smart Miami club you would expect to be filled with beautiful people. But on one hot summer evening in 1978, the only things it contained were blood and horror.

It was Sunday 23 July 1978. North Miami's prosperous Sixth Avenue neighbourhood was quiet. The elderly man approaching the ritzy World of Health Spa had no inkling of the horror he was about to uncover. The lights were on but the main door was locked. The old man knew that the owner, his son, usually left a side door open when he was working, and he went in that way.

Just inside the door, he found the bloodspattered body of his son. John Mitchell, aged 33, had been shot several times. His keys lay beside the body; it looked as though he had been trying to escape from his killers. The old man rushed to a phone and, with trembling fingers, he called the police. It was just before 9 p.m.

Uniformed Metro-Dade officers were on the spot within minutes. They made a quick search of the building to see if there was anybody else on the premises. The first thing they found was that the club's office had been ransacked – maybe a robbery had gone wrong? However, it soon became clear that robbery was the least of their worries.

In a pool of blood

Sprawled naked in a pool of her own blood in a back hallway of the club lay the body of an attractive young blonde. She had been shot in the head and throat. Her clothes were scattered nearby. Moments later the body of a clothed woman in her 30s was discovered. She had been shot to death in one of the whirlpool bathing rooms.

By this time, Ronald Wright, the Deputy Chief Medical Examiner, had been called and Metro homicide detectives Charles Zatrepelak and Robert Derringer were assigned to lead the triple murder investigation.

First they had to establish who was involved. They knew one of the victims was the owner of the club, John Mitchell, and questioning the father gave the investigators some idea of his last-known movements.

It was Mitchell's habit, even on his days off, to go to the club to help shut up shop for the day. The plush gym with its lavender carpeting needed careful cleaning, and he liked to supervise the job. It was doubly important today, since a new cleaning crew was due to start work at 4 p.m. when the club closed. He had left home at about 3.30, telling his wife Linda that he'd be back for dinner.

When he had not returned after four hours, Linda Mitchell started to worry, especially as it was his daughter's birthday. At about 8.30 p.m., she phoned her father-in-law, who lived near the club, to ask him to find out why her husband was late. As a

John Mitchell's office had been ransacked. Were the three brutal killings simply the product of a robbery which had gone wrong?

A curious crowd gathers behind police crime ropes, craning to see inside the spa

The Miami News - MICHA?

Police hunt motive in spa triple murder

ARY MATERA,
OANNE HOOKER
nd HELGA SILVA
Miami News Reporters

Two women found shot to death last ht inside a posh North Miami Beach alth Spa were identified today as an 8-year-old Miramar High School grad- ate and a North Dade woman who re- tly started her own cleaning service

women. The spa is described as catering to upper-class health-seeking clients and had a "wide range of exercise and weight-reducing equipment.

One woman was identified as Patricia Lynn Beck, 18, of 7500 Shalimar St., Miramar, whom her mother said had graduated in June.

The other was identified as Carol Ra- duazzo, 34, of 1152 NE 196th St., who had started a cleaning business six to work

the spa after police arrived said Mitchell often stayed after doing to help clean up and little if any money was kept there.

Steve Beattie, who operates a karate school next door and also was a partner of Mitchell, said he thought this was the first time Mitchell had hired women to clean the spa; "It was always guys be- fore."

Richard Raduazzo, brother-in-law of the slain Carol Raduazzo, said her busi- ness was "just beginning to mushroom into something big" and she normally not do the cleaning her work her-

"she had to, she k,"

Above: Crowds of North Miami residents gather outside the World of Health Spa as news of the murders spreads.

result he made the first dreadful discovery.

Linda arrived at the World of Health Spa at about 11.00 p.m. There she was com- forted by her husband's friend Steve Beat- tie, who had apparently just heard the news. Scots-born Beattie, who had a repu- tation as one of the toughest men in Florida, drove through the police cordon, and had tried to force his way into the build- ing. He was part owner with Mitchell of a martial arts studio in the same building.

The two female bodies were quickly identified as Carol Raduazzo, aged 34, and 18-year-old Patricia Lynn Beck. Friends

The club was usually fairly busy on Sundays, with members of the body- conscious Miami community working out and using the spa facilities.

and relatives could think of no reason why any of the victims had been killed.

Raduazzo had set up an office cleaning business about six months before, and had just won a contract to clean John Mitchell's World of Health Spa. She did not normally do the cleaning herself, but on this occasion an employee had been off work, and Raduazzo had taken her place.

Patricia Beck had been employed by Raduazzo as a part-time cleaner. Beck, who had just graduated from Miramar High School, had no career plans and was doing temporary work over the summer to make some money.

Police questions

Police investigators had a number of questions. Were the killings simply a means of silencing witnesses to a robbery attempt? Alternatively, was the ransacking of the health club's office an attempt to dis- tract attention from a planned killing? If it was a planned killing, who was the prime target? And why was the youngest victim found naked, but without any signs of sexual assault?

Before going into the health business, John Mitchell had owned or part-owned massage parlours in Fort Lauderdale, Miami and Hialeah, but he had never been charged with law-breaking. In any case, for the last four years he had had nothing to do with the sex business, and had a clean record.

Without evidence, police could make no guesses. However, the bloody scene was soon sealed off by police crime scene search specialists and by technicians ▶

Beattie talks to victim Mitchell's wife at scene of crime

Above: John Mitchell's wife was comforted at the murder scene by a friend called Steve Beattie. Nobody could have foreseen the part he was to play in the investigation.

Right: Patricia Beck, recently graduated from high school, was the youngest of the three victims.

Below: The club had been expensively built and needed careful cleaning. Patricia had been one of the cleaning crew.

from the Dade County Public Safety Department Crime Laboratory.

One thing which immediately caught the eye were the dozens of cartridge cases strewn all over the club. "They were of at least two different calibres," one detective reported. "Some appear to have been fired by a .38 Special or a .357 Magnum revolver. The others are .25 calibre, probably from a small semi-automatic pistol."

Random shooting

The indiscriminate spraying of bullets led the detective to add: "It doesn't have the appearance of being a professional hit."

One item that aroused some interest was a piece of chewing gum which was stuck to Patricia Beck's skin. This was taken away for analysis, in the hope that teeth impressions could be found or that the blood type of the killer could be established. However, the dental impressions were too indistinct. The biologists managed to detect various components of blood-type A saliva, but as Patricia Beck

was type A it could have been her own gum.

While the scene was being photographed, and criminalists began the search for forensic evidence, one of the lab's most experienced crime scene technicians set to work. Eddie Stone had encountered the confusion usual at the scene of any multiple murder. Once things settled down, fingerprint specialist Stone decided to see if he could develop a fingerprint from the body of one of the victims. It was a technique that Metro-Dade had been trying out for the past year, but with little or no success. However, conditions in this case looked promising.

Prints from a body

After drawing a blank with the bodies of John Mitchell and Carol Raduazzo, he turned to the naked body of Patricia Beck. This time, he got a result. As Stone applied the black fingerprint powder to the victim's lower calf, three prints became evident. These were photographed *in situ*, then 'lifted' from the skin. The two outer prints were somewhat blurred, but the central impression was clear. The prints were then rushed round to the Crime Lab's Identification Section, to begin the process of trying to find a match.

Once the medical examiner had declared the victims dead and the preliminary scene-of-crime investigations were complete, the bodies could be removed for post-mortem examination. This was carried out the next afternoon and revealed

Above: Patricia Beck and her employer Carol Raduazzo had just started to clean the spa when they were shot. Police investigators found their cleaning equipment scattered over the floor just where they had dropped it.

Above and inset: Carol Raduazzo had only been operating her cleaning business for a matter of months when she was murdered near the health spa's whirlpool bath.

that the victims had generally been in good health, and that none of the bodies showed any evidence of drug or drink intake.

Cause of death in all three cases was assessed as gunshot wounds, with a best estimate of time of death being between 4.30 and 6.30 p.m. This agreed with the last time any of them were seen alive, by one of the club's instructors who had left the building at 4.15 p.m.

John Mitchell had been shot seven times in the body and neck. One of the wounds, a shot that smashed through the victim's arm and into his abdomen, was surrounded with powder marks, indicating that the bullet had been fired from close range.

Patricia Beck had been shot twice, once in the neck from relatively close range, and once in the abdomen. Carol Raduazzo died from a single shot through the temple.

Surprise suspect

The investigation took a new and surprising turn two days after the killings. The Crime Lab's Identification Section came up with a match to the fingerprint from Patricia Beck's leg. The print was from the left middle finger of Steve Beattie, the friend of the family who had comforted Linda

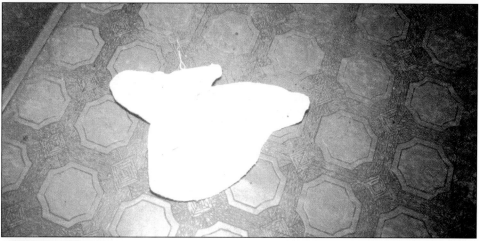

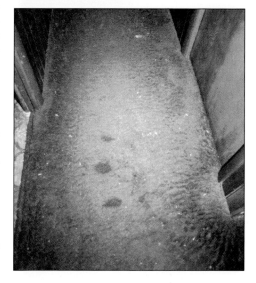

Above and left: Scene-of-crime investigators had plenty of evidence to sift through, ranging from Patricia Beck's clothing to hallways strewn with blood and cartridge cases. While these indicated the sequence of events, much more would have to be found to identify the murderer or murderers.

Mitchell on the night of the crime! Just to make sure, the Dade County technicians sent copies of the scene-of-crime print and of Beattie's prints to the FBI, who confirmed that they matched.

The police knew quite a lot about Steve Beattie. He was well known in the Miami area as a karate champion, part-time celebrity bodyguard and extremely vicious nightclub bouncer. He had been arrested several times in the previous 10 years, ▶

Skin print

Below: Scene-of-crime photographers record the position of the body of the youngest victim. There appeared to have been no sexual motive in her slaying. Why Patricia Beck was found naked, with her clothes strewn about the corridor, remains a puzzle.

The State of Florida's case against Steve Beattie hinged on the single identifiable fingerprint found on the body of Patricia Beck.

By the summer of 1978, the Dade County Public Safety Department Crime Laboratory had been attempting to get usable prints from the bodies of murder victims for about a year. Unfortunately, skin is not a very good medium for retaining fingerprints, and if the skin is covered with clothing or body hair the chances of getting a result are remote.

Eddie Stone, senior Crime Scene Technician for Dade County, was on call on the night of 23 July 1978. Arriving at the scene of the triple slaying in the World of Health Spa, Stone began his search.

Searching for clues

He started with the two clothed victims, dusting the areas of exposed skin, but with no results. However, the third victim was more promising. Stone realised that the environment and conditions were conducive to developing a latent fingerprint. The air-conditioning ensured that the skin was dry, most of the body was free of blood, and as the victim had been a teenage girl there was no body hair to get in the way.

Obtaining a fingerprint from skin is not easy: skin is often wet or greasy, and clothing or body hair will disrupt any evidence. Two of the bodies in the World of Health murders were fully clothed, but one was naked and dry. The chances of success were good. Sure enough, on dusting Patricia Beck's leg evidence of fingerprints emerged.

usually on charges of assault and battery or aggravated assault.

It was not difficult for the police to lay their hands on their suspect. When the karate champion's name entered the frame, the investigating officers were in the process of conducting interviews with all of the friends and associates of the victims. Suspecting nothing, Beattie came in to police headquarters at midday on Tuesday 25 July.

After answering questions for an hour and a half, Beattie was surprised at being charged with the triple homicide. He denied all the charges but admitted to having been at the health club on the day of

the murders.

According to his first story, he had left at about 1.30 p.m., only returning after the bodies had been found. After more questioning he changed his story, saying that he had been at the club at 5 p.m. and had stayed for five minutes. He claimed he had seen nobody.

Suspicious alibi

Beattie stated that he had been with a friend for most of the day, and that the friend would provide him with an alibi, which he did. However, since nobody else could account for the pair's movements and

the police felt that two people were involved in the killings, the second man immediately became a suspect, although in the absence of any proof he was not arrested. Significantly, the friend fled the country two days later.

Police now obtained a warrant and searched Beattie's home in the hope of finding the murder weapons. No guns or rounds of ammunition were found, but they did confiscate several items of clothing and a pair of sandals, which were taken away for forensic analysis.

The sandals were found to have microscopic traces of blood and skin attached. The blood was type A, like that of Patricia Beck, and the skin was similar to hers.

Beattie continued to protest his innocence, but now the investigators found a possible motive for the killings. John Mitchell had been sole owner of the World of Health Spa, but had a half share in Beattie's karate school that operated in a back hall of the club. Beattie and Mitchell had each taken out $100,000 insurance policies

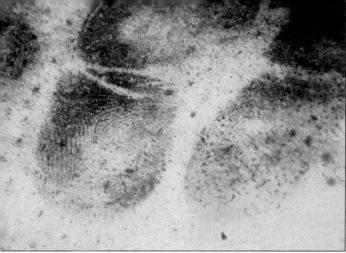

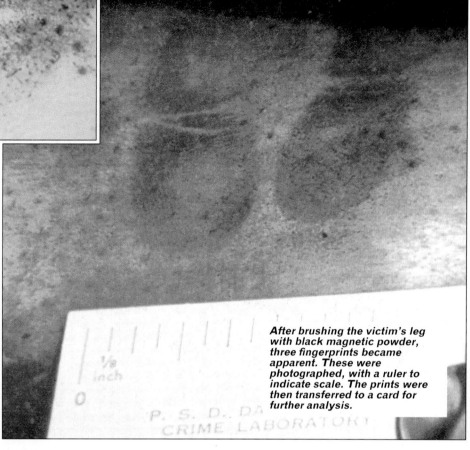

Once the prints had been photographed in place, they were lifted off with sticky tape and transferred to record cards.

Eddie Stone started at the head, making a visual search for latent fingerprints in the blood which covered it. Seeing nothing, he treated the head and upper body using glossy Kromekote cards. These are very smooth and shiny cards which are pressed to the skin, lifting any prints which may be present on to the card. The Kromekote is then processed with magnetic powder, producing a second-generation mirror image of the original print.

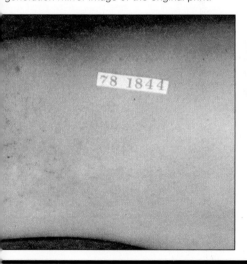

After brushing the victim's leg with black magnetic powder, three fingerprints became apparent. These were photographed, with a ruler to indicate scale. The prints were then transferred to a card for further analysis.

The Kromekote having produced no result, Stone moved on to the lower body and legs. This time he brushed fingerprint powder directly on to the smooth, dry skin, using a fibreglass filament brush.

Within a couple of seconds of dusting the legs, Eddie Stone noticed three latent fingerprints begin to appear on the victim's calf. The three prints, by this time six or eight hours old, were photographed *in situ* with a ruler to give scale. They were then lifted with transparent adhesive tape, and transferred to a fingerprint backing card.

Although the outer prints were indistinct, the middle print was usable. That single print, the first ever successfully lifted from the body of a murder victim, was the state's sole piece of hard evidence against Steve Beattie. It was enough to convince the jury, and Beattie was found guilty of triple murder.

A detective follows a scene-of-crime examiner – overalled and booted to prevent evidence contamination – into one of the murder rooms at the spa.

on each other's lives. Detectives believed it was that $100,000 which had cost John Mitchell his life, and which had resulted in the deaths of two innocent witnesses to the crime.

The trial

The case came to trial in December 1978. Although the defence managed to persuade Beattie's friend to come back and testify, they had an uphill struggle. Beattie's attorneys had no answer to the damning forensic evidence, particularly the fingerprint taken from the naked body of Patricia Beck.

Beattie made a dramatic plea at the end of the case, insisting that the jury find him completely innocent or completely guilty, thus cutting off any chance his lawyers had to bargain for a guilty plea to a lesser crime.

The jury took the hard man at his word, and found him guilty of first degree murder, which carries a mandatory death sentence.

Beattie was given three consecutive death sentences: consecutive because, if they were ever commuted to life imprisonment he would have to serve a minimum of 25 years for each murder. This would mean a minimum of 75 years, so that he would never come out of prison alive.

In court, Steve Beattie had almost seemed to welcome the death sentence. His first day on Death Row changed his mind. All of a sudden, the 'toughest man in Miami' wanted to live. His lawyers asked for a new trial, but it was denied.

Beattie's bravado wore thin, and in August 1981 he had had enough. Somehow he smuggled enough sleeping pills into his cell for an overdose. He died, alone, on Sunday 9 August.

His epitaph was a comment from Sergeant David Rivers of the Metro homicide department.

"It's no great loss."

Biography

The Hard Man

Scots-born Steven Beattie was the son of a professional boxer who moved to Canada with his family when Steven was seven. He and his brothers grew up tough. One brother was a successful professional boxer, becoming world lightweight champion in the late 1950s. Another brother took his struggles to a different stage and was elected to Canada's House of Commons.

Steve went a different route. After being convicted of car theft in Canada in 1962 and serving a month in jail, he moved south to the warm sun and easy life of Florida. As soon as he reached Miami he got involved in a number of violent means of employment, on one occasion being matched in a prize fight with a gorilla.

Karate champion

Powerfully muscled, Beattie was five feet 10 inches tall and weighed 180 pounds. He had taken up martial arts in his teens, rising to be a fifth degree karate black belt by the time he was 20. He won the Florida State karate championship in 1962, a title he was to hold for the next three years.

However, his approach to the sport led to a falling out with his own teacher.

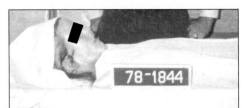

Steve Beattie's victims would have had a lot going for them had they lived. Carol Raduazzo had just started her own cleaning business; Patricia Beck had the whole of her adult life before her; and John Mitchell's health club was a successful money-spinner. But thanks to one man's greed, all three ended up on a mortuary slab long before their time.

Right and below: Steve Beattie's reputation as a hard, violent man brought him into regular contact with the police. However, the events on Sunday 23 July 1978 went a long way beyond mere violence. With the brutal gunning down of three innocent people, Steve Beattie became a triple murderer.

Former State Karate Champion Charged in Health Spa Deaths

FROM PAGE 1A

in the same time span. All were shot to death. Beck's was nude. Her clothing, un-...ed, was scattered on the floor ...er body.

BEATTIE, of 2730 N. 72nd Ter., ollywood, who operates a karate ...ool next door to the health spa, ...d the charge, Metro Homicide ...ry Hancock said. Late Wed-...ay afternoon Beattie still was ...he homicide offices, conferring ...th lawyer Irwin Block, who ar-...ved at 2:25 p.m. Block said he had ...t represented Beattie before.

Beattie was booked at 5:58 p.m. ...Dade County Jail on three ...of first-degree murder and ...rge of using a firearm to ...a felony.

...is scheduled to appear at an ...bond hearing today in Circuit ...Block filed a subpena with ...cuit Court clerk's office late ...sday for homicide Detective ...Derringer to appear at the

...ll the people have been com-...wn (to headquarters) for ...'s," Hancock said. "Every-...talked informally before, ...y had anything relevant, ...edge of the victims, they ...ed to come down for for-...ements."

DETECTIVES, Hancock added, ...no reason to suspect Beattie ...Wednesday, when they be-...satisfied that the "physical ...ce," which they would not ...linked him directly to the

...ling.

...Ve still haven't established a ...: for this thing," Hancock ...Police plan to go over the spa's ...ess and financial records as ...vestigation proceeds.

...lice would not say whether ...thought that Mitchell, Beck or ...azzo was the prime target of ...two-gun attack. One weapon is ...257- or ...lieved to have bee...

Steve Beattie as Pictured on Tropic
... has wide reputation as tough

Is He The Toughest Man in Town?

Beattie, a Scot who emigrated with his family to Canada when he was a child and came to South Florida in the early 1960s, was well-known in local police and bartending circles as one of the area's toughest lounge bouncers. He had worked at, among other places, the Castaways and the Newport and several years ago was assistant manager at Honey For The Bears, a popular Coconut Grove discothe-que.

...zine, which called him "The ...est Man in Town." He was th... karate champion between 1... 1965.

He was arrested June ...on a charge of aggravate... The charge, filed after a... tween Beattie and a secu... at an apartment building... ...ped for lack of prosecut... was accused of beating ...uard after an argu... at the Sun... 184 NW 1...

"I disassociated myself from Steve," said Johnny Pachivas. "He was the only one of my students I couldn't get on with. I didn't like his behaviour. He hurt people intentionally. He beat up little people in bars. I don't teach that."

By night Beattie was building up a reputation as an extremely tough nightclub bouncer. He established what were called 'Tiger Squads'; teams of the toughest bouncers in town who could be hired to clean up troubled clubs — fast.

"A lot of enemies"

"He made a lot of enemies," a fellow karate expert said. "In bars, he was notorious for pushing a guy's girlfriend to start a fight. He didn't use a whole lot of tact in handling trouble."

As Beattie's reputation grew, he began to take jobs as a bodyguard to visiting celebrities. At the same time, he was of great interest to the police. In 1967 he was charged with assault and battery. In 1969 it was assault, battery and rape. In 1976 he was arrested for aggravated battery. None of the charges stuck, either because of people withdrawing complaints or through lack of evidence.

Beattie set up his own karate school, which was how he got into business with John Mitchell. Although his students thought highly of him, fellow instructors were less complimentary. One commented: "I teach martial arts as a virtue, and I don't think he had that. You are supposed to better yourself, not become better than others."

DNA CATCHES THE KILLER
of Candice Williams

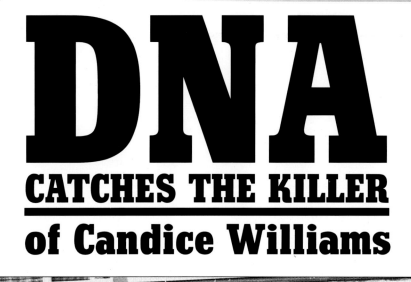

Above: Candice Williams was a schoolgirl who lived in the Erdington area of Birmingham. On Monday 24 July she and her sisters, together with two other girls, went to the Perry Common Recreation Ground, about a mile from Candice's home.

The murder of 13-year-old Candice Williams in 1978 was a mystery. But advances in forensic science in the 1980s meant that her killer was brought to justice years later.

The law rarely reaches back in time to punish crimes committed years ago, and most murders are solved within days or weeks rather than years. But more than 12 years separated the brutal rape and murder of 13-year-old schoolgirl Candice Williams and the eventual conviction of her killer.

During those years the techniques of forensic analysis underwent a revolution with the introduction of DNA profiling. Using the sophisticated new identification technique on forensic samples kept on ice since July 1978, the policemen and scientists involved were able to close the book on a long-unsolved case.

Candice Williams was born in Birmingham on 20 June 1965, the youngest of five children. Her mother died at the end of May 1978, just before Candice's 13th birthday. She was a slender girl, with her father's West Indian colouring, and wore her thick hair in a bushy Afro style.

The school summer holidays were in progress, and on the morning of Monday 24 July Candice was at home in Montpelier Road in the Erdington district of Birmingham. She had fish and chips for lunch, and then went out with her sisters, Wendy and Regina, to visit a friend, leaving home at about 12.30 p.m. At about 2 p.m. the three sisters, together with two other girls, walked about a mile to the Perry Common Recreation Ground, where they remained until about 3.30 p.m. Then, following an argument, Candice walked off and left the park and headed towards Erdington. It was the last time she was seen alive by anyone except her murderer.

About 500 yards from the Perry Common Recreation Ground is Wyrley House, a 12-storey block of council flats. In 1978 most of the flats were occupied by elderly people. They had lifts to reach the first 11 floors, but the 12th floor, and the roof above it, were only accessible by means of

Wyrley House is a couple of minutes' walk from Perry Common. On the afternoon of Tuesday 25 July, one of the residents found Candice's body on the stairway leading from the top floor to the roof of the block of council flats.

staircases.

At about 2.40 p.m. on Tuesday 25 July, Arthur Poulton, a 64-year-old resident of a 12th floor flat in the block, decided to check out the stairway to the roof. Sometimes down-and-outs slept rough on the landing halfway up the stairway.

Mr Poulton found no sleeping drunks, but what he did find was infinitely worse. Sprawled on the landing was the body of a young girl, hardly more than a child. Poulton called the emergency services, and before long a police constable was waiting with the body until a police doctor officially confirmed the girl's death. The officer then accompanied the body to the Birmingham Central Mortuary where, later the same day, Robert Williams identified his youngest child, Candice.

Strangled with her shoelace

After the identification, a Home Office pathologist carried out an autopsy which revealed that Candice had been strangled by means of a ligature - one of her shoelaces – around the neck. Several swab samples were taken, to be examined by experts at the Home Office Forensic Laboratory in Birmingham, and Dr Nicholas Prance, who examined them, was able to establish that human semen was present.

Hairs found at the murder scene were studied with the aid of a comparison microscope, which enables the user to identify minute differences between two images. In this way, hairs from any suspect could be closely compared with those from the scene of the crime: differences in colour and overall morphology would enable the investigators to narrow any suspect list down by a process of elimination. One hundred and fifty samples from suspects were examined in the course of the next two years.

Her last meal

Forensic examination of stomach contents revealed the potato material from Candice's last fish-and-chip lunch. Dr Prance also discovered fragments of a fleshy yellow fruit, probably a peach. Later a greengrocer recalled that on Monday 24 July a young man aged about 20 had come into his shop to buy two peaches. Outside the shop a young girl seemed to be waiting and, shortly afterwards, the greengrocer saw the young man with his arm around the girl. He pointed the couple out to an acquaintance, as the young man resembled his own son.

A police team of up to 40 officers worked from the incident room set up at Erdington police station, carrying out a large number of house-to-house enquiries, street questionnaires and a comprehensive check on all known sex offenders. The local press co-operated in mounting a massive coverage, and there were radio and TV appeals for information. By December 1978 the investigating team had taken almost 950 statements, carried out over 2,500 individual interviews and seen over 7,000

Semen, hair and DNA

The police investigation team was headed by Detective Chief Inspector Ernie Robinson (centre). He was assisted by Detective Inspector Peter Higgins (right) and forensic scientist Dr Nick Prance (left).

Samples of semen taken from Candice Williams' body showed that she had been the victim of a sexual assault. By establishing the attacker's blood type from the semen, and by testing for one of 10 different forms of a type of enzyme found in blood, investigators should have been able to eliminate nine out of 10 suspects. Unfortunately, the swab traces in the Williams case were sparse, and were contaminated with extraneous matter. Dr Nicholas Prance, a forensic biologist from the Home Office Laboratory in Birmingham, decided to keep the samples on ice until more sophisticated tests were evolved. This was very far-sighted, because in the next 10 years the development of DNA testing would enable forensic scientists make an identification which was totally impossible in 1978.

Candice had been strangled with one of her shoelaces. Samples taken from the body also revealed that she had been sexually assaulted.

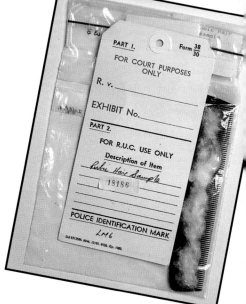

people. No arrests were made.

On 3 August a man named Patrick Hassett had been interviewed during the house-to-house enquiries: police had discovered that in the early hours of Monday 24 July, the day of the murder, Hassett had been arrested, drunk, and charged with the attempted theft of a lorry. According to his own account, given in the interview on 3 August, he left Thornhill Road police station after being charged on the Monday morning, and went to see his solicitors in the city centre, getting home around 3 p.m. He claimed he then slept until about 5 p.m., tried unsuccessfully to find his girlfriend, Pamela Sambrook, at her house nearby, returned home, and then went out at 5.30 p.m.

Hassett's alibi

According to his story, Hassett then drank at the Witton public house in Aston, and played pool with three unknown Irishmen until 9 p.m. He had then gone to another pub, the Stockland in Stockland Green, to carry on drinking with two brothers, John and Jimmy Malone, until 11 p.m., when he went home to bed. On the next day he stayed in bed until 2 p.m., going to see Pamela Sambrook at 3 p.m.

Hassett's account of his movements was full of uncheckable periods, but was not followed up, as he was not an immediate suspect. But two years later, events conspired

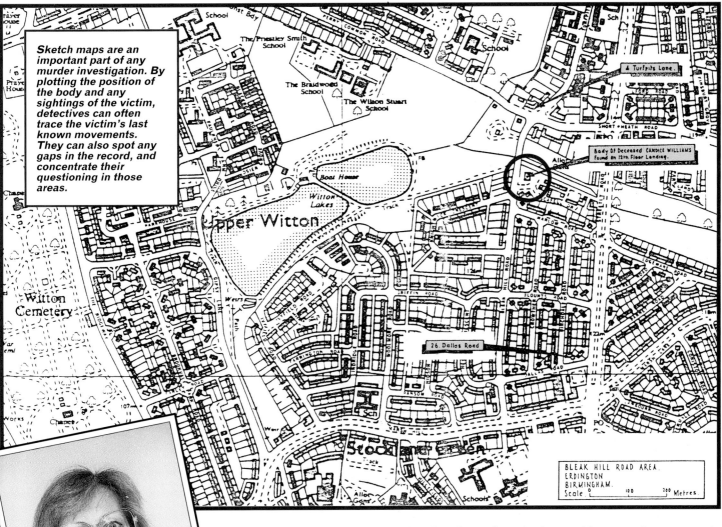

Sketch maps are an important part of any murder investigation. By plotting the position of the body and any sightings of the victim, detectives can often trace the victim's last known movements. They can also spot any gaps in the record, and concentrate their questioning in those areas.

A former girlfriend of a man called Patrick Hassett brought him to the attention of the police more than two years after Candice had been killed.

to put him in the frame for the first time.

In 1980 there were two vicious rapes of young girls in the Erdington area, in January and November. Press speculation linked these rapes with the murder of Candice Williams. Eventually a man totally unconnected with Hassett was convicted of the two rapes, but during the time of intense press speculation, Hassett's ex-girlfriend decided to go to the police.

In her statement on 21 November 1980, Pamela Sambrook said that a day or two after the report of Candice William's murder, Hassett came round to her flat. He had marks on his neck like cat scratches and claimed to have received them through being roughed up by the police. It was soon obvious that he wanted an alibi. He said the police would be coming to see her, and that he wanted her to back up his story that he had been with her at the time of the murder. She had told him that she would not lie to save him.

Lack of evidence

As a result of Pamela Sambrook's statement Hassett was arrested on 3 December 1980, and body hair and saliva samples were taken by a police surgeon. Hassett's hair samples were compared with those found at the scene of the crime. There seemed to be microscopic differences, but there were also enough similarities for Hassett to remain a prime suspect. But in the absence of further corroborating evidence, he was released.

In 1983 Hassett was sentenced to 18 months' imprisonment for another assault. And soon after his release he was arrested for a particularly brutal assault on a 12-year-old girl in Tamworth. This conviction occurred at about the same time that the successful development of DNA profiling was being reported.

Hassett's new conviction brought the focus back on to him as a prime suspect in the Candice Williams case, and he was interviewed in July 1985 at Shrewsbury Prison by members of the West Midlands police. He angrily denied the offence, and was unco-operative.

When a convicted criminal is in prison, he is in the custody of the Home Office, and not the police. The police may request, but not demand, intimate body samples such as blood, hair and saliva for forensic analysis. Only when the prisoner is in police custody can samples be taken by force, if they are refused – and then only head hair may be taken, as long as this is carried out by a police surgeon.

On 5 July 1988 Detective Chief Inspector Ernest Robinson and Detective Inspector Peter Higgins visited Patrick Hassett at Wakefield prison with a view to obtaining samples which could be used for DNA profiling. News of important advances in forensic science travels fast in the criminal world, even in the confines of prisons. Hassett was well aware of his vulnerability to a DNA profile match-up, and was also conversant with the constraints placed on the police by the rules of the Police and Criminal Evidence (PACE) Act regarding police powers inside prisons.

Hassett refused to give intimate samples and requested legal advice. The next day, in the presence of a solicitor, he

rally

n the application to Coun.
th today.

r. Marriner, who is un-
ployed, said that if the meeting
s banned it would be switched
a secret venue in London on
same date.

David Perris, secretary of
gham Trades Council, said
night that he was "horrified"
he prospect of the British
ement being allowed to use
Town Hall.

is not an issue of free
in Birmingham's premier
place, but a highly
ive application which
use violence."

IAL COMMENT — Page 4

Hunt for killer of girl, 13

A girl, aged 13, was found murdered in a Birmingham block of flats yesterday.

Candice Williams, of Montpelier Road, Erdington, had ... sexually ...

found by ...ley House, ...d, Erding-... 3 p.m. It ...se leading ...or to the ...

...her died ...

IN THE POST TOMORROW

Poaching explained

Learn how to be an ...

Father retraces girl's last steps

By MICHAEL ORR
Birmingham Post Police Reporter

A grief-stricken father yesterday retraced the last steps of his daughter murdered in a Birming-ham tower block, two months after the death of her mother.

Clutching the hand of his son Boris, Mr. Robert Williams walked round the recreation ground where his 13-year-old daughter Candice had been playing until she ran off on Mon-day.

...walked ...
...Hou...

Police have now re-opened the files on two other cases where young girls were accosted in the same area — the last only seven days ago.

The first case happened at the beginning of the month and Mr. Meffin said both were "of a sexual nature." He appealed for anyone who may have been simi-larly accosted and had not reported it t... ...olice to come forw...

Ever...   the
flats   wed
and   ice

The investigation was a massive affair, with thousands of interviews being carried out and extensive coverage in the local press. But police did not get a break in the case until years later.

again refused to provide any samples.

There was nothing the police could do about this state of stalemate except wait out Hassett's sentence. On 20 February 1991 Patrick Hassett was released from Wakefield prison on the completion of his sentence, and was promptly rearrested by DCI Robinson and DI Higgins. They in-formed him that he was being taken to Erdington police station, where he would be requested to supply intimate samples. If he refused, head hair would be taken by force if necessary.

Hair samples

After consulting his solicitor Hassett re-fused to give intimate samples, but did agree to head hair samples being taken. The police surgeon duly took these, and they were forwarded to the Birmingham Forensic Science Laboratory for DNA pro-filing. Hassett had to be bailed in accord-ance with PACE, and was due to surrender to his bail at 10 a.m. on 14 March 1991. DCI Robinson bet DI Higgins a steak dinner that Hassett would not turn up on the date.

Dr Nicholas Prance had moved on to the

Huntingdon Forensic Science Laboratory by this time, and the hair samples were processed by Mark Webster in Birming-ham. The matching of the hair sample with the profile from the original swabs was a painstaking task, due partly to the sparse-ness and low quality of the originals, and partly because the taking of profiles from hair is more difficult than from a straight-forward blood sample – which, of course, Hassett had refused to give, claiming an allergy to needles.

DNA profiles are matched by lining up sequences of dark bands appearing on X-ray film to see if any of them coincide. Mark Webster achieved a matching that gave the statistical probability of someone other than Hassett being the attacker as one in 3,200. This would not have been good enough as evidence in a court of law, so further work was carried out to try to in-crease the odds.

The first technique used on Hassett's hair had been of a type known as a multi-locus probe. A different technique, known as a single-locus probe, was now

Evil Mind

Violent record

If computers had been available to detectives in the 1970s, instead of clumsy card indexes, Patrick Hassett would have been a suspect much earlier. Born in March 1959, his first indecent assault, on an eight-year-old-girl, occurred when he was only 12 years old.

There was not enough evidence to hold him in the Williams case, but in 1983 Hassett was sentenced to 18 months' imprisonment for dragging a woman into his car and assaulting her.

Horrific assault

Soon after his release in 1984, when Hassett was working as a builder's labourer in Tamworth, he subjected a 12-year-old schoolgirl to an horrific attack. Easily caught, after a woman heard screams from his van and took the registration number, Hassett was sentenced to 10 years at Stafford Crown Court on 28 February 1985.

Investigators began to tie Hassett into the unsolved Williams case again. But the problem was proving it.

Above and right: Patrick Hassett had been one of many people questioned at the time of Candice Williams' murder, but he did not become a major suspect until two years later. Released because of lack of evidence, he again came into the frame in 1984 when he was convicted of an assault.

employed, and eventually produced estimated odds of about one in 12,000 that anyone apart from Hassett could have produced the semen on the original swabs.

DI Higgins won his steak dinner from DCI Robinson when Hassett surrendered to his bail on time, and was charged with the murder of Candice Williams. The trial began on 3 March 1992, with Hassett pleading not guilty. As in all cases where DNA profiling is used in evidence, it was the prosecution's job to convince the jury that the DNA evidence was a reliable indicator of guilt.

DNA evidence

To demonstrate the complexities of his evidence to the court, Mark Webster hired a video set-up with an overhead camera.

Mark Webster's testimony bore fruit. The defence's expert witness began by challenging the validity of the DNA evidence, and ended up finally admitting that it did look as if Hassett was guilty.

On 18 March 1992 Patrick Joseph Hassett was found guilty by a majority of 10 to two of the murder of Candice Williams in July 1978. He was sentenced to life imprisonment, convicted by the evidence of his own body.

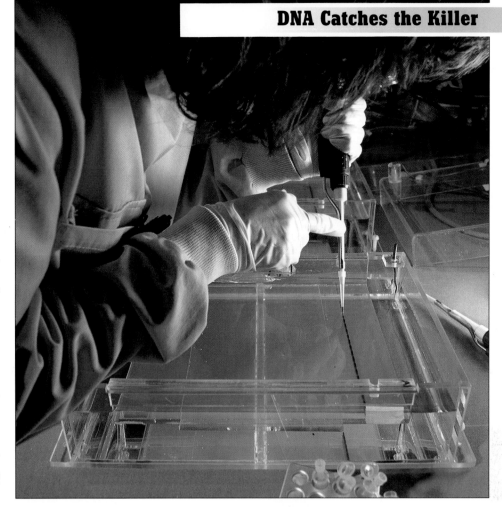

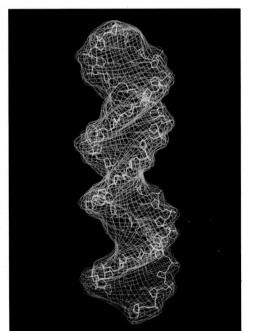

Above: While Hassett served his sentence for the attack in 1984, Dr Alec Jeffreys of the University of Leicester developed his revolutionary DNA test. Even in its early days, this could link microscopic samples of biological material with one particular person with almost complete certainty.

Left: DNA analysis of the semen swabbed from Candice Williams' body was compared with samples taken from Patrick Hassett's hair. The tests showed that the semen was 12,000 times more likely to have come from Hassett than from anybody else.

Right: Robert Williams had to wait a long time for justice to catch up with the killer of his daughter.

BETRAYED BY HIS BITE

She had been an early settler in Florida's Dade County, and for most of her 77 years she had helped the local community. But Margaret Haizlip's life came to a brutal end when she took pity on a drifter and invited him in for a sandwich.

Margaret Haizlip was a conscientious woman, always on time for her voluntary job at the Good Shepherd Day Care Centre in Homestead, Florida. When she failed to turn up on the morning of 23 February 1979, one of her co-workers drove to her house at 9790 Wayne Avenue in nearby Perrine to check that everything was all right. Mrs Haizlip was not particularly frail, but she was 77 years old, and had lived alone since being widowed 10 years before.

When she got to the house, the young teacher realised something was wrong. Mrs Haizlip's car, a 1952 blue and white

Right: Seventy-seven-year-old widow Margaret Haizlip was one of the earliest residents of the Florida community of Perrine, having moved there as a teenage bride in the 1920s.

Below: Mrs Haizlip lived alone in this comfortable but modest home. A pillar of the local community, her murder came as a terrible shock.

Chevrolet, stood in the drive, its bonnet up. The front door of the house was unlocked and the lights were on. Frightened to go in, she asked a nearby shopkeeper to check. What he found sent him running back to his hardware store, shouting "Call the police! Someone's been murdered!"

The police were there within minutes. Mrs Haizlip's battered body lay on the bedroom floor. She had been kicked and punched repeatedly – eight of her ribs were broken and her skull was fractured – strangled with the flex from an electric iron that was lying beneath her body, and raped.

What appeared to be a bruise on the victim's hip turned out on closer examination to be a bite mark, although it had not broken the skin. A dental expert said the bite came from an upper set of teeth. At first, detectives theorised that the woman

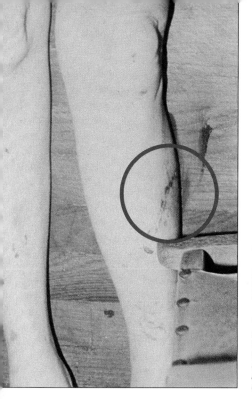

Too many suspects

The police had plenty of suspects at the start of the investigation, most of them suggested by neighbours, who had seen a surprising number of apparently suspicious characters around the Haizlip house the evening before the murder.

Neighbours' reports

Several people reported seeing two men in a run-down old Chevrolet cruising aimlessly around the neighbourhood. Others reported a teenager who used to ride a red bicycle around Perrine in the early hours of the morning; he was already suspected of several burglaries, including one at 9790 Wayne Avenue. A teenage passerby reported seeing a black youth with what looked like a stick lurking in nearby bushes, while a neighbour said she had seen a white youth with blond hair call at Mrs Haizlip's front door earlier the previous evening.

Suspects eliminated

The police concentrated their efforts in the immediate area, and managed to trace and question all these suspects, but they were ruled out by the forensic evidence. The blond hair ruled out the black youth, while none of the other suspects showed the distinctive gap visible in the bite pattern in the baloney.

The victim had been mercilessly battered, raped, and strangled by an electric cord. A wound on the victim's hip was at first thought to be a bruise. On closer examination, however, it was revealed to be a bite mark, inflicted on the body after death.

may have rolled on to her own denture plate, which had been dislodged by her beating, but the two did not match in any way. Besides, the wound was consistent with having been caused after death.

There was no sign of a forced entry, and no-one could have entered the house without doing some damage. Mrs Haizlip had been burgled several times – she had once chased a teenage intruder out of the house by threatening him with a frying pan – and had had two or three locks fitted on every door.

Detectives developed three theories. One was that she had caught someone trying to steal her car, and he had forced her back into the house and attacked her. Another was that she had got up early, as was her habit, and opened the door to let the cool air in and her killer had simply walked in off the street. The third possibility was that her attacker was someone she knew and trusted.

Time of death

Time of death evidence was inconclusive, but the strong suspicion was that she had been killed in the early hours of the morning. Local residents told police that all the dogs in the neighbourhood had begun to bark around 5 a.m.

Crime lab technician Tom Carroll made a methodical search inside and outside the house. He found that the tip of a knife had been broken off in the Chevrolet's ignition, and that the wires had been pulled out as if someone was attempting to hot-wire it. When Carroll held the wires together, the engine roared into life.

He vacuumed every room, using a fresh bag for each, and labelled them for later examination. He also collected together the torn remnants of the slip Mrs Haizlip had been wearing and itemised everything else that had been disturbed in the otherwise clean and tidy house. On one of the twin beds in the room in which Mrs Haizlip was found, Carroll discovered a long, blond hair.

He took photographs of the scene and lifted more than 80 latent fingerprints. He even tried using a recently-developed technique to lift fingerprints from the body, but without success.

He had better luck with his search in the kitchen. The cooker was set a few inches out from the wall to make room for the gas pipe. On the floor behind the cooker, Carroll found some slices of baloney, pressed together as they would be in a vacuum-sealed packet. The meat was fresh and not dusty, so presumably had not been there for long. Someone had taken a bite out of the slices before dropping or throwing them behind the cooker. Carroll took photographs of the bite marks back at the crime lab. They clearly showed a gap between the lower front teeth, something that the victim's dentures did not have.

Evidence

Who bit the baloney?

When Margaret Haizlip's body was moved, crime scene technicians discovered one of her dentures on which she had been lying. By comparing it with the baloney sausage found later, they were able to show that the bite marks on the food did not belong to the victim.

The crime scene search of the Haizlip home produced some partly-eaten baloney sausage. The bite marks in the meat were not made by the dead woman's dentures. Bite marks are highly individual, and can be almost as conclusive proof of identity as a fingerprint. If a matching set of teeth were found, then they probably belonged to the killer.

Once all the scene of crime evidence had been processed, the police had impressions of both sets of the killer's teeth, his fingerprints, his blood type (from the semen found on the body) and perhaps his hair colour. They would be able to identify him easily once he was in custody, but had no idea who he was or where to look. Then, on 17 March, three weeks after the murder, they had a huge stroke of luck.

An anonymous informant called the police to say that a Ford Thunderbird parked on Wayne Avenue had 200 pounds of marijuana stashed in its boot. As a pair of detectives pulled up behind the Thunderbird, it drove off. They followed it to a hamburger restaurant, then ushered the driver and his female companion out of the car so that they could search it. There was no bale of grass in the boot, but there was a small bag of it on the front seat where the woman had been sitting. The pair were arrested and taken in for questioning.

At the station, the woman said she had information about the Haizlip case. She lived across the way from the murder house. She told police that a man called Roy Allen Stewart had visited her two weeks after the killing and confessed that he had done it.

Stewart had lived at the house before she moved there, and had at one time worked with her boyfriend. She also knew him as a regular at the bar where she worked. Stewart had a consuming interest in drugs, she said, particularly cocaine, and was often short of money. He had told the woman that he had killed Mrs Haizlip when she caught him stealing.

She had not informed the police at the time because there was an outstanding warrant against her for forgery and because of the drugs angle. She did not know where he was, but she had heard he had moved to South Carolina.

Killer identified

Stewart had a record in both South Carolina and Florida. The police dug out a set of his fingerprints and found a match for two of those they had found at the scene of the crime. They had their man.

Stewart was traced to Columbia, South Carolina, 700 miles from Perrine. He had moved there around the time Margaret Haizlip had been killed. He was staying with an aunt and uncle, and worked for a local roofing firm.

He was arrested and extradited back to Florida on 20 April. Under questioning, he claimed that Mrs Haizlip had asked him in for a sandwich, and that he had attacked her when she saw him pocketing a watch.

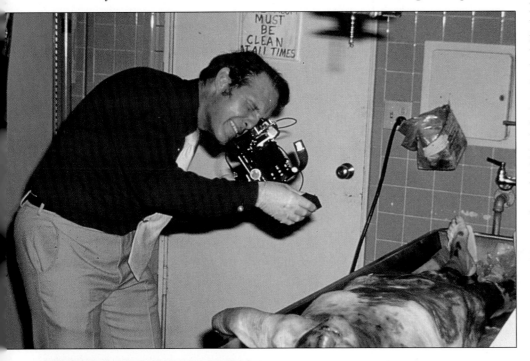

Above: A police photographer records the position and extent of the wounds on the victim's body. Accurate photographs of evidence are vital in criminal investigations. In the case of Margaret Haizlip, photography enabled forensic dental specialist Richard Souviron to record and analyse the bite mark on the victim's body.

Devout Christian

Margaret Haizlip and her husband, James, were one of the Perrine's founding families. They arrived in 1920, when a land boom was transforming the sub-tropical swampland at the southern tip of Florida into the city of Miami, and there they raised their son and daughter and took an active part in Perrine's affairs. Margaret worked as a teacher, and she and her husband were both stalwarts of the Methodist Church and the American Legion.

Sunday School teacher

James Haizlip died in 1967, but his widow continued to live in the family home on Wayne Avenue, teaching a Sunday School class and working five mornings a week with four- and five-year-old children at the Day Care Centre. Her own children had moved away, and urged her to join them, but she chose to stay in the family home as the community she had helped establish decayed around her, losing its small-town identity as it was gradually absorbed by the lawless sprawl of Miami.

There was only a small amount of disturbance in the living room of the Haizlip house. However, crime lab technician Tom Carroll managed to lift a number of latent fingerprints. Most of the 80 he found belonged to the victim, but several had been left by the killer.

Sausage slice slip-up

At Stewart's trial, the most damning evidence against him came from dentist Dr Richard Souviron. He testified that the bite marks on Mrs Haizlip's hip and on the half-eaten slices of baloney sausage the police found behind the gas cooker were both made by the accused.

On 14 May, Souviron took an impression of Stewart's bite at his dental surgery in Coral Gables. He then used this to make a cast of Stewart's teeth, in the same way he would if making a crown or a partial denture. He then used this cast to 'bite' into 20 samples of baloney and compared the impression with those on the slices of sausage found at the scene.

Teeth match bite marks

Photographs of the cast and of the bite marks in the sausage and on the murdered woman's hip were put under a comparison microscope and matched in every detail. It was this that led Souviron to claim that there was "reasonable dental certainty" that Stewart had made both bite marks.

This was the first time dental evidence of this type had been used in a criminal case in Florida. A few weeks later, Souviron received nationwide publicity when he presented similar evidence at the trial of serial killer Ted Bundy, who had left bite marks on the body of one of the two University of Florida students he had killed earlier that year.

Above: The breakthrough in the case came after a drugs bust. One of the people arrested named the killer of Mrs Haizlip as Roy Allen Stewart. Stewart, from South Carolina, had a long drugs-related criminal record.

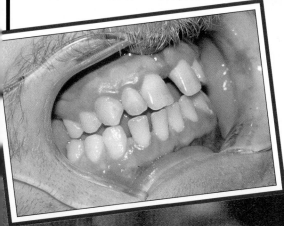

Left: Stewart was picked up by police in South Carolina. He had a noticeable gap in his teeth, just like the bite marks recorded at the scene of crime.

The detectives were inclined to disbelieve this story. It did not explain the evidence of the attempted car theft. They also knew that the confession would be challenged in court. The fingerprint evidence was not watertight, either. Stewart knew Mrs Haizlip, and could have left them on a previous, legitimate visit.

The only evidence that could not be explained away was that of the bite marks, and the defence team knew it. Almost a whole day of Stewart's trial was taken up in legal arguments about the admissibility of the dental evidence.

Dental evidence

At the end of this, Judge Lenore Nesbitt ruled that the bite evidence was as acceptable in evidence as fingerprints: "It appears to me that the method of bite comparison is a standardised procedure, and there is no reason it should be rejected." A dental expert accordingly testified that there was "reasonable dental certainty" that Stewart had bitten the victim and the three slices of sausage.

Stewart was found guilty on Monday 2 July. In accordance with Florida law, the jury of six women and six men returned three days later to decide on a penalty; they recommended the death sentence. Stewart was also sentenced to life for rape, 30 years for armed robbery (he had a knife in his pocket when he entered the house, though he didn't use it) and 15 years for burglary.

Various appeals have failed, and Stewart is currently awaiting execution on Florida's Death Row. ☐

Roy Stewart was charged with first-degree murder and came to trial at Dade Circuit Court in June 1979. It was one of the first American cases in which bite mark evidence was ruled admissible. Found guilty, Stewart was sentenced to die and is currently on Death Row.

Police conduct house-to-house enquiries at the Bedfordshire village of Edlesborough after another vicious assault by the rapist dubbed 'The Fox'.

HUNTING 'THE FOX'

A brutal rapist was breaking into homes at the dead of night. But he left behind a trail of forensic evidence.

Armed police search Linslade Wood near Leighton Buzzard. The Fox used a sawn-off shotgun in his attacks – and he was quite prepared to use it if his victims resisted.

Detectives called it the rape triangle. In the summer of 1984 a sex attacker struck repeatedly around Leighton Buzzard, Cheddington and Dunstable. The masked rapist struck in the dead of night, attacking his victims in their beds. Armed with a sawn-off shotgun, he would break into a house and find his way to the bedroom. Several couples were woken at gunpoint, the men were tied up and the women assaulted.

Detectives dubbed the attacker 'The Fox' after he broke into a house while the occupants were out. He moved furniture into the middle of a room and covered it with a bedspread to form a crude 'lair'. He gathered ties, dressing-gown cords and shoe laces, ready to tie up his victims. But when the young couple who lived at the house came home, his nerve failed him and he fled.

Others were not so lucky. The Fox got into another house on 9 June and threatened a businessman and his wife at gunpoint in their bed. The husband flung himself at the intruder and the gun went off in the struggle. He had one of his fingers blown off and the rest of the shot blew a hole in the bed, narrowly missing his wife. The attacker fled into the night.

But his reign of terror was not over: he attacked three other couples during July.

Each assault was more vicious than the last, but, although The Fox tried to cover his tracks, he was leaving a trail of forensic evidence behind him.

The Fox went to ground for over a month, but then on the evening of 16 August he decided to drive north to his home town of Sunderland. The next day was his 32nd birthday and he thought it would be nice to spend it with his mother.

As he drove his yellow Austin Allegro along the M1, he was suddenly overcome by the powerful urges that had already turned him into a monster. As he approached the junction of the M1 and the M18 in south Yorkshire he spotted the lights of the farming village of Brampton en le Morthen. He had put one of his shotguns and some cartridges in the boot of his car just in case.

Good opportunity

It was 2.45 a.m. The opportunity seemed too good to miss. Traffic was fairly light on the motorway at that time and so he pulled on to the hard shoulder. When he thought the coast was clear he reversed his car into a small clump of trees just off the motorway. He snapped off some saplings to cover the distinctive vehicle, gathered up his shotgun and mask from the boot and set off to the village.

At the first house he earmarked to attack he was forced to make a hurried retreat when two fierce dogs started barking. But across a field stood another house that seemed to offer a good opportunity. The Fox's luck could not have been better. The family who occupied the building had had decorators in the previous day. A downstairs window frame had been painted and left open to dry. Swiftly and silently The Fox was in the house.

In a bedroom a 41-year-old man and his wife were asleep. As he pulled the bedclothes off them their nightmare began.

Both were tied up and their attacker threatened to shoot if either uttered so much as a word of protest. As in a previous attack, two small children slept in an adjacent room, mercifully unaware of the terror being carried out a few yards along the landing.

The rape triangle

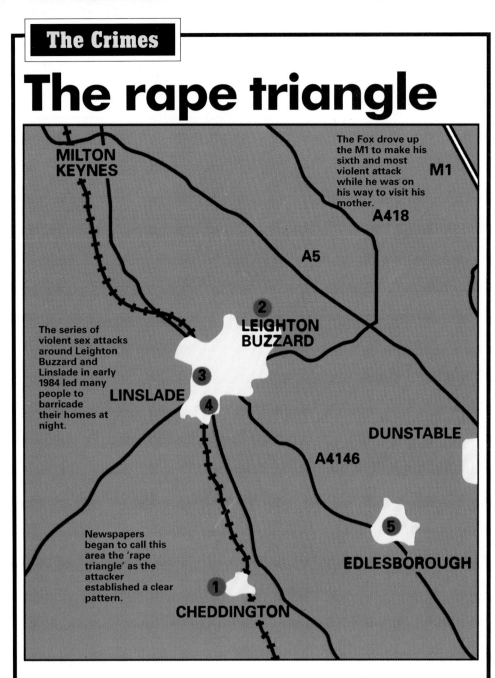

The Fox drove up the M1 to make his sixth and most violent attack while he was on his way to visit his mother.

MILTON KEYNES

M1

A418

A5

②

LEIGHTON BUZZARD

The series of violent sex attacks around Leighton Buzzard and Linslade in early 1984 led many people to barricade their homes at night.

③

LINSLADE

④

DUNSTABLE

A4146

⑤

EDLESBOROUGH

Newspapers began to call this area the 'rape triangle' as the attacker established a clear pattern.

①

CHEDDINGTON

1 The reign of terror began when a man was sexually assaulted at gunpoint in Cheddington.

2 A businessman was shot as he defended himself and his wife against a masked intruder in their home.

3 A couple were tied up at Bideford Green, but the wife's screams caused their armed attacker to flee.

4 Another couple in the same area were unable to resist and the wife was assaulted.

5 A woman and two men were assaulted in a house at Edlesborough. During the prolonged attack The Fox stood on a standard lamp, leaving a clear impression of his shoe.

Left: The Fox tried to cover his tracks, but police discovered vital forensic evidence at the scene of several attacks.

Right: Police hold a press conference in Dunstable. Public alarm inside the 'rape triangle' was leading people to take steps to defend themselves.

Army spy kit used in ambush

During the hunt for The Fox police set up one of the most elaborate high-tech traps ever in the search for a serial criminal in the UK. After the discovery of the attacker's secret hiding place for his car following the Brampton incident, detectives thought he might be tempted to return to the same place again.

Infra-red cameras

After a thorough search, police installed a hidden infra-red remote-control camera, capable of giving pin-sharp images, even at night, trained on the copse. Sensors to detect movement and sound were borrowed from the army, and a team of camouflaged officers lying in wait were given night-sight binoculars to keep watch in total darkness.

Meanwhile in the Buckinghamshire/ Bedfordshire 'rape triangle' up to 300 officers a night hid out in gardens, parks, potting sheds and shrubberies hoping to catch The Fox red-handed.

In the end, all the traps failed and The Fox was captured by old-fashioned elimination of suspects.

Policemen using military night sights lay in wait for The Fox night after night. These amplify the available light, giving a clear picture even on a dark night. Since the rapist kept attacking houses in the same area, there was some hope he could be caught red-handed.

A police helicopter joins in the search around Edlesborough after the rapist attacked a house in the early hours of the morning.

The Fox believed he had thought of everything to prevent getting caught. Before leaving the bedroom he took a hairbrush from the dressing-table and carefully brushed through his victim's body hair to remove all traces of himself.

Forensic clues

Then he took a sharp knife from his pocket and carefully cut out a large square from the bottom bedsheet which had been soiled with semen. He put the knife, brush and portion of bedsheet in his pocket, slipped out of the house and hurried through the dew-soaked meadows back to where he had hidden his car.

He thought he had been smart. But he had just made a series of catastrophic mistakes. In the cold light of day detectives were able to follow his tracks away from the village to the spot where he had hidden his car.

Along the trail they found a patch of recently dug-over earth and leaves. One team of officers started to dig, while the second team followed the footprints in the long grass. The diggers were quickly rewarded. Wrapped in a plastic bag was his sawn-off shotgun, still loaded and cocked ready to fire.

The second search team were quickly in luck, too. Only 300 yards from the house where the attack had taken place they found the hairbrush and the piece of sheet. A hurried attempt had been made to hide them, but it had not been good enough.

At the spot where the car had been hidden there were tyre tracks and more footprints. The detectives were sure the spot would yield more important forensic clues. The hiding place among the trees was a gold mine of evidence. But with traffic flashing past on the motorway just yards away, the detectives had problems. They didn't want to inconvenience thousands of drivers by closing the motorway, and they wanted to disguise what they were doing in case the man they hunted passed by again.

In co-operation with the traffic branch they found the perfect solution. They

Self-defence

Panic rush to buy guns

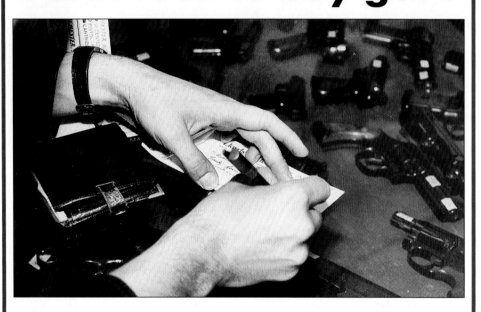

The Fox's rampage spread so much fear around Leighton Buzzard, Buckingham and Linslade that shops selling security locks and window bars sold out. Security companies reported a flood of orders for burglar alarms and the police were swamped with applications from people wanting shotgun certificates. A gunsmith sold out of shotguns and ammunition and then sold his entire stock of air weapons to local residents anxious to protect their homes and families.

Armed and ready

Hysteria grew so bad that police were called to a series of accidental shooting incidents – luckily none causing death or injury. In one incident police rushed to a house near Leighton Buzzard where a householder had let fly with a shotgun

In the so-called 'rape triangle' householders began to arm themselves in case they were targeted by the rapist. Applications for shotgun certificates were at an all-time high. Those who already had them stocked up on ammunition.

through his kitchen window because he thought he he had heard The Fox creeping outside. Police discovered the noise had been made not by The Fox, but by a pair of mating hedgehogs!

In Britain the courts often take a very hostile attitude to people who defend themselves with firearms. If someone had driven off The Fox with a shotgun, they would probably have been sent to prison as well.

staged an accident as a cover for the real reason for their activity.

The inside lane was coned off and police cars with warning lights flashing parked on the hard shoulder. Two or three damaged cars were brought from a nearby repair yard and two ambulances were also borrowed to add authenticity to the scene.

Police searchers even dressed in paramedic-style green jump suits as they sifted through the dirt and rubbish on the edge of the motorway.

Hidden glove and mask

It didn't take them long to discover more major clues. Before driving away The Fox had dumped a glove and his mask. He had hoped the two items would not stand out among the other rubbish and dirt that littered the edge of the motorway. But he hadn't bargained on the police tracking down his hidden parking spot so quickly.

The glove had rabbit-skin lining. Microscopic tests were later to prove that it was an exact match with tiny pieces of fur found at the home of his first victim. And better still, it was an exact match with shreds of fur found adhering to material he had used to bind a victim in one of his attacks in Leighton Buzzard.

The mask had been made from part of an overall or boiler suit. A leg had been cut off, knotted at the top and eye holes made in it. But the best was still to come. Forensic officers patiently examining the crushed and broken vegetation where the car had been parked found tiny specks of paint sticking to a broken sapling. Each was no bigger than a pin head. In the lab under a microscope the tiny slivers could be clearly identified as a car paint known in the motor industry as harvest yellow. The only company using that colour paint was British Leyland.

Sick fantasies fuelled by porn

Hard-core pornography is believed to have twisted Malcolm Fairley's simple mind and turned him from a minor league burglar into a violent sex maniac. When detectives searched his home they found a collection of pornographic videos, many of them illegal Continental imports, featuring bondage and extreme sado-masochism.

During his confession Fairley had openly told detectives and psychiatrists how many of his sex crimes had been inspired by scenes from blue movies. And he revealed that part of what drove him to sex at the point of a gun was a belief that he had a very small penis.

Passing sentence, the judge, Mr Justice Caulfield, remarked how Fairley had lived out his sex-film fantasies via his crimes. He told him: "You are a decadent advertisement for evil pornographers. You are one of the worst casualties."

Referring to the psychiatric reports on Fairley, he told him: "Every single one of these reports refers to the influence of pornography on you."

Right: Like many convicted rapists, Malcolm Fairley had a huge collection of pornographic material hidden away in his house.

So now the police knew The Fox drove a British Leyland model. But finding the right car from the thousands made would be an impossible task. However, more help was on its way. After the story of the Brampton attack hit the papers a lorry driver came forward. He had been on the M1 going north that morning and had seen a car backing into the woods at the M18 junction. Unfortunately he could not remember the make or colour.

Would he submit to hypnosis, the detectives urged? The trucker agreed. He described an Austin Allegro. He couldn't remember the registration, except he knew it was a Durham number. But he could remember the colour. It was harvest yellow.

Detective Chief Superintendent Brian Prickett, leading The Fox hunt from his HQ in Dunstable, knew he was tantalisingly close to nailing his man. Yet in another way he was still a million miles away.

Suspect's description

His team had built up a clear picture of their suspect. They knew his age, build, shoe size, blood group, accent, the car he drove, and more.

They were sure he was left-handed. Several victims had described their attacker as wearing his watch on his right wrist, usually a sign of a left-hander. They even knew he had a passion for salted peanuts, after several victims had described him stealing bags of the snacks from their larders while ignoring other goodies. In fact, the CID had even codenamed the hunt 'Operation Peanuts' because of this.

In many ways they knew *what* he was. They just didn't know *who* he was.

They were also amassing important scientific clues they knew would be vital when he was found. From the first attack in Cheddington a scene of crime officer had taken a cast of the marks made on a wooden window frame when it was forced with a heavy screwdriver. If the suspect still had such a screwdriver when he was caught it could be matched perfectly against the frame. From an attack at Edles-

Malcolm Fairley is led away after a brief appearance at Dunstable Magistrates Court. Trapped by good detective work, he confessed his crimes when he saw the wealth of evidence against him.

Oseney Crescent, they were both taken aback to see a man cleaning a car outside the address. The man was Malcolm Fairley, the car was a harvest yellow Austin Allegro. Only days before they had attended a briefing where they had been told about the scientific breakthrough stemming from the scraps of paint on the tree in Yorkshire.

Fairley was actually polishing the car as the detectives approached. When they introduced themselves Fairley seemed unfazed. But while they talked Henkes couldn't help noticing some scratches on the paintwork that he thought could have come from scraping against a tree.

Setting a trap

Then he spotted something that gave him a flash of inspiration. On the dashboard he saw a watch. "Do yourself a favour," he told Fairley, "put your watch on, if you leave it there someone will nick it."

Fairley smilingly obeyed, strapping the watch to his right wrist – the sure sign of a left-hander – and the wrist on which The Fox's victims had said their attacker wore his watch.

Henkes was now sure this was The Fox, but he needed something else and suppressed his mounting excitement.

Above: The Fox was arrested by DC Dick Henkes (left) and DC Nigel Tomkins (right).

Left: Fairley and his wife had just moved to their new flat in Kentish Town when he was arrested.

borough they had found a clear impression from one of The Fox's shoes where he had stood on the base of a standard lamp.

The pressure didn't let up. Shortly after the Brampton rape there had been two incidents at Peterlee in County Durham. A young woman asleep in bed had woken to find a masked intruder in her room. When The Fox tried to rape her she had fought back fiercely, giving him a painful bite on his little finger and screaming until he fled.

Animal urges

Still driven by his animal urges, he promptly drove to the other side of town and broke into another house. As he got in he was confronted by a woman and her daughter. The older woman fainted, her daughter screamed, and The Fox was put to flight again.

Now the local police were offering all the details via computer links to the Dunstable incident room. It certainly looked like the same man.

On 9 September the attacks switched south again. A woman was attacked by a masked intruder at her home in Bradwell near Milton Keynes. She had been slightly injured with a knife while fighting off her attacker, who had fled into the night. But though no-one knew it then, The Fox had only two more days of liberty left.

The investigation team had considered thousands of possible suspects. Hundreds had already been eliminated.

On Tuesday 11 September, two young detective constables, Dick Henkes and Nigel Tompkins, both attached to the squad, were told to carry out another routine check on a possible suspect.

As part of their enquiries the police had asked hundreds of doctors, social workers and other professional people to supply them with lists of any newcomers to the Bedfordshire/Buckinghamshire border area.

A doctor in Aylesbury had sent in details of a man who had recently registered with him after moving down from the Sunderland area and renting a flat locally. The man was called Malcolm Fairley and a check with police records showed he had some previous convictions for burglary. But that was all. The squad had already checked and eliminated dozens like him.

Police visit

Fairley had already moved on from Aylesbury and had taken another rented flat with his wife in Oseney Crescent in the Kentish Town area of north London.

Henkes and Tompkins were told to go to see him. It was a low priority job: so low they could not even have a CID car. The investigation had already cost over £1 million and their boss, Chief Superintendent Prickett, knew he couldn't waste a penny of his force's budget. The young detectives were told to take the train – second class.

As Henkes and his partner walked along

Betrayed by

Fairley started his life of crime as a burglar. He was an experienced house-breaker by the time he turned to rape. But the tools he used to break into his victims' homes all left distinctive marks, which would help send him to prison for life.

Below: Fairley's sawn-off shotgun and some of the ammunition were recovered near the M1 at Brampton.

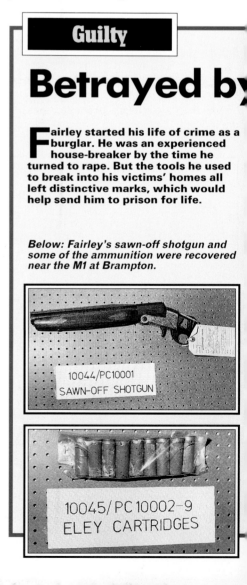

10044/PC10001
SAWN-OFF SHOTGUN

10045/PC 10002-9
ELEY CARTRIDGES

He asked if he could check the boot of Fairley's other car, a Ford Capri. There was no doubt. Inside was a pair of blue overalls with one leg missing. Henkes took Fairley's wrist and slipped on the handcuffs. The Fox had been run to ground.

At Dunstable Fairley put up little resistance when questioned by Detective Chief Superintendent Prickett and his right-hand man Detective Inspector Sid Roscoe. After being shown the wealth of forensic evidence the police had amassed against him, he was soon confessing everything.

"I can't help myself . . ."

He told the detectives: "I can't help myself. I got into the habit of it. It just went on and on and got worse and worse. It just weren't the real me."

Fairley's trial was held at St Albans Crown Court on 26 February 1985. He pleaded guilty to 12 charges, including three counts of rape, two indecent assaults, two counts of burglary with intent to commit rape and five charges of housebreaking.

He was sentenced to six life sentences, plus 14 years for the burglaries, 10 years for an indecent assault on a farm manager and two years for an indecent assault on a

74-year-old woman at the beginning of his reign of terror.

The judge, Mr Justice Caulfield, told him: "There are degrees of wickedness and depravity beyond the capacity of condemnatory description. Your crimes fall within that category – crimes for which there is no exculpation, crimes which left your victims in utter terror and with life-long burdens of terrifying memories. You

Right: Malcolm Fairley, 32, pleaded guilty to three counts of rape plus other offences.

desecrated men and women, old and young, in their own homes, which you then pillaged."

A life of crime

After Fairley had been arrested police discovered a man who was not so much a fox but in many ways a frightened mouse. The small-time nature of his true criminal self was best underlined at his trial when, as well as the main charges, he asked for another 68 burglaries to be taken into consideration.

Bullied at school

Fairley, the youngest of nine children, was born in the Durham mining village of Silksworth in August 1952. A speech defect made him shy and introverted. At school his lisp and slight build made him a target for bullies and he left at 15 unable to do even simple arithmetic and barely able to read and write.

He had already been in trouble for theft while still at school and he was in more trouble for a series of petty thefts and burglaries soon after leaving.

He married for the first time when he was 19, but his wife walked out after two years because of his violence towards her. Two years later he met his second wife, Georgina, with whom he had three children.

In and out of jail

During the next 10 years he was in and out of jail for burglary. After he was charged with the rapes he told Detective Chief Superintendent Prickett: "I am sorry I did, but I am glad, too, because now I can get treatment to help me."

His defence counsel, Michael Connell QC, in his plea of mitigation for Fairley, told the court: "He has only a very limited understanding of the wickedness of his actions. His personality and physical defects have caused him to be more susceptible to evil influences such as pornographic videos."

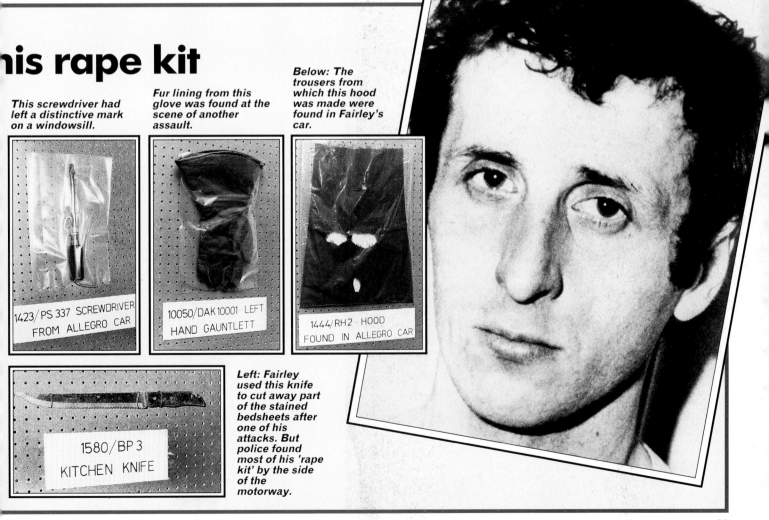

his rape kit

This screwdriver had left a distinctive mark on a windowsill.

1423/PS 337 SCREWDRIVER FROM ALLEGRO CAR

Fur lining from this glove was found at the scene of another assault.

10050/DAK 10001 - LEFT HAND GAUNTLETT

Below: The trousers from which this hood was made were found in Fairley's car.

1444/RH2 - HOOD FOUND IN ALLEGRO CAR

1580/BP 3 KITCHEN KNIFE

Left: Fairley used this knife to cut away part of the stained bedsheets after one of his attacks. But police found most of his 'rape kit' by the side of the motorway.

THE HEADLESS, HANDLESS

Above: It looked fairly innocuous: a gleam of white off a deserted road in the San Bernardino Mountains of California. But a second look revealed that it was a body.

Left: The remains were those of a middle-aged woman, and the body was partly naked. But that was not all: it had been mutilated beyond recognition.

In a gruesome murder case in California in the late 1940s, the identification of the victim seemed impossible. The body's head and hands had been chopped off.

A motorist driving from San Bernardino into California's Mojave Desert in January 1946 spotted a gleam of white just off the road. Investigating, he was horrified to discover the corpse of a middle-aged woman, half naked and with its head and hands roughly hacked off.

It was pure chance that had led to the discovery of the corpse. The Rim of the World road is a bleak, wild place. Running through the San Bernardino Mountains surrounding the town of San Bernardino, it is largely desert and scrub land. Lonely box canyons lead from the road deep into the hills. Under normal circumstances it might have been months before anyone discovered the remains, by which time the weather and wild animals would have converted them into scattered bones.

The sheriff of San Bernardino County was called to the scene. Preliminary examination could shed little light on the identity of the body, thanks to the brutal mutilation it had undergone. Without a head there was no face to be recognised, and the removal of the hands had also removed the fingerprints. The clothing found with the body offered no clues, and neither did a blood-flecked tartan blanket found nearby.

Shooting victim

One thing was clear, however. The victim had been shot. Post-mortem examination extracted two bullets from the body. They were .32 calibre, almost certainly fired from an 'automatic' self-loading pistol. The victim had died less than 10 hours before the body was found.

The only option open to the investigators was to look through the missing persons' files. This took some time, but after three weeks the name of Dorothy Eggers was turned up. Eggers had been reported missing by her husband Arthur at about the time the body was found. At 41, she was the right sort of age, but according to the missing person's report she was slimmer and taller than the victim.

Fifty-two-year-old Arthur Eggers was a mild-mannered clerk. Notably quiet in person – he had been given the nickname 'Caspar Milktoast' – he was not well matched with his wife Dorothy. She was a fun-lover. According to her husband, she had habitually hitch-hiked to nearby towns in search of the excitement he had been unable to provide. When he reported her disappearance, Eggers suggested that she might have picked up the wrong man.

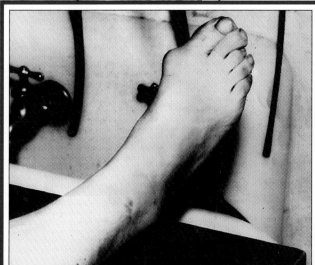

Left: One identifiable feature of the body was its feet. If the chiropodist who had treated this bunion could be found, a name could be given to the victim.

Below: Arthur Eggers identifies the body of his missing wife, Dorothy.

Without a head or hands, police had nothing with which to identify the body. They could tell it was a woman of average height, slightly overweight and probably in her 40s or 50s.

After three weeks the San Bernardino sheriff's office had eliminated all likely identities, so they turned to less likely ones. To their surprise, a clerk named Arthur Eggers identified the body as his wife Dorothy. Eggers had reported his wife missing but, according to the description he had given, Dorothy had been a taller, thinner woman. Why had he given a false description?

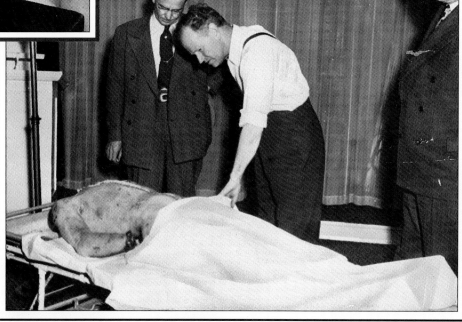

CORPSE

But if the body was indeed that of Dorothy Eggers, why did she not match the description on the missing person's report? Almost immediately the police discovered that the description Eggers had given of his wife was false. Dorothy was shorter and plumper than he had said – in fact, she was of the same build as the body found in the mountains.

It seemed a long shot, but the investigators had no other leads. Eggers was called to the mortuary, where he stated that the body was indeed that of his wife. Further confirmation was provided by a doctor who had treated Dorothy for a painful foot condition. He recognised her bunions.

So why had Arthur Eggers given police an erroneous description of his wife? He had no reason to lie. Unless, of course, he was trying to put them off the scent of a crime. Could it be that he knew more about the death of his wife than he was letting on? It was certainly suspicious.

Car yields clues

Then a second suspicious circumstance arose. Eggers had recently sold his car. The buyer, a deputy sheriff, noticed some curious spots in the trunk. Spots that looked uncommonly like dried blood. Hearing that there were some doubts about Arthur Eggers, he reported his findings to his superiors. Added to the false description, this was certainly enough to hold Arthur Eggers while further enquiries were made, so he was arrested.

After several days of questioning Eggers confessed to the murder of his wife, saying that he had lost his temper in

Blood in the trunk

Arthur Eggers was already under suspicion after his misleading description, but there was not enough evidence to detain him. However, a week after his wife went missing, he had sold his car. The buyer was a San Bernardino deputy sheriff, and he noticed some spots that looked like dried blood in the car. When Eggers identified his wife the deputy remembered the spots, and forensic tests showed that the blood was human.

an argument about her going out with other men. He said that he shot her and disposed of the body while their two adopted children were out at the movies.

Eggers said that he did not know what he had done with the head and hands, but he vaguely remembered burning them. However, he later changed his story several times, and eventually completely retracted his confession. Instead he claimed that his wife had probably been murdered by a casual lover.

Solving the case

With only a retracted confession to work with, the San Bernardino sheriff did not have enough to make a charge stick: he had to find hard evidence tying Eggers to the death of his wife. But San Bernardino County did not have the resources to mount a major murder investigation. Fortunately, the city of Los Angeles lay only 60 miles to the east, and the Los Angeles Police Department had the experience and expertise to crack the case. At that time, Californian forensic investigators led the world in the use of science to solve crime.

The mild-mannered wife killer

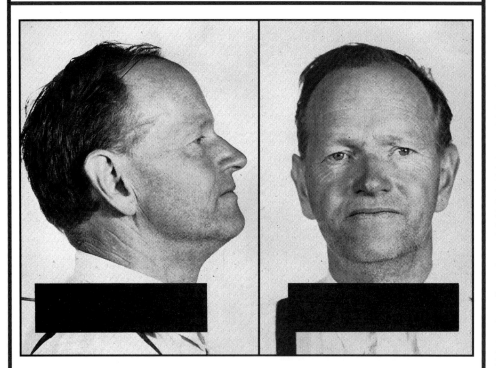

It would be difficult to find a less likely murder suspect than 52-year-old Arthur Eggers, but the evidence against him was substantial. And as the police investigated the family background, they soon found a possible motive. Arthur had been dominated for many years by his more extrovert wife. They were a mismatched couple: Dorothy Eggers was very much a party animal, who regularly hitch-hiked to nearby towns in search of action and excitement. She was promiscuous and regularly ridiculed her husband's sexual inadequacy. Perhaps it had all come to a head. Maybe after all the years of baiting, Arthur had finally snapped, and his hidden anger had culminated in murder.

Criminal investigator Ray Pinker was assigned to the case. His first task was to analyse fragments of bone found in the Eggers' incinerator. These turned out to be of animal origin.

The next step was to have a closer look at the items found with the body. The tartan blanket was identified by the Eggers children as coming from their home. The blood on the blanket was of the same type as the body's, and also matched the stains found in the trunk of the car bought from Eggers by the deputy sheriff.

Pinker also found some loose strands of hair that looked identical to samples taken from Dorothy's hairbrushes. The blanket was then examined in filtered ultra-violet light to check for the presence of semen. None was found, which put paid to Eggers' theory that his wife had been killed by some casual lover.

Ballistic tests

A search of the Eggers family home revealed a self-loading .32-calibre pistol. Pinker test-fired it into a wooden chamber packed with cotton waste, then retrieved the bullet and compared it with the murder bullets under a comparison microscope. They were fired from the same gun.

The final evidence against Arthur Eggers came from his tools. Eggers was a keen amateur carpenter, and had a full set of equipment. After Eggers' arrest Pinker analysed many of the implements, and one of the saws was found to have minute parti-

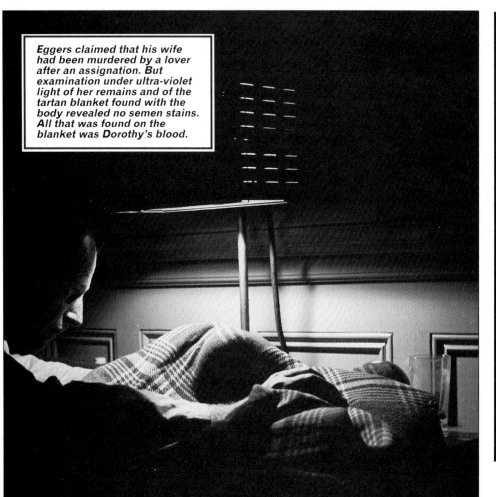

Eggers claimed that his wife had been murdered by a lover after an assignation. But examination under ultra-violet light of her remains and of the tartan blanket found with the body revealed no semen stains. All that was found on the blanket was Dorothy's blood.

Finding the murder

1 Although the body of Dorothy Eggers had been brutally mutilated, this was not the cause of death but an attempt to prevent identification of the corpse: Dorothy had actually been shot. Two .32-calibre bullets were extracted from the body during the post-mortem examination. On searching Eggers' home, a .32-calibre automatic was found. Forensic scientist Ray Pinker test-fired the gun to check if it was the murder weapon.

cles of human blood, flesh and bone caught between its teeth.

When Arthur Eggers came to trial for the murder of his wife in the summer of 1948, the forensic evidence gathered by Ray Pinker was overwhelming. The jury was unanimous in its decision that Eggers was guilty, and he was sentenced to death.

Lasting mystery

Arthur Eggers, the mild-mannered clerk, died in the gas chamber at San Quentin prison on 15 October 1948. To the end, he kept the secret of what he had done with his wife's head and hands. They have never been found. □

Human flesh on the saw

Forensic scientist Ray Pinker examines one of Arthur Eggers' saws. Pinker was able to identify tiny particles of human flesh and blood caught between the saw's teeth.

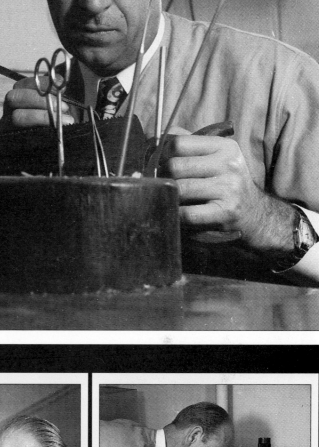

Police only had Arthur Eggers' unsupported confession that he had killed his wife. In order to secure a conviction, the investigators had to find hard evidence that Eggers had mutilated his wife's body. Post-mortem examination of the body showed that the bones had been severed by a saw. Eggers was a keen amateur carpenter and handyman and had a full set of tools, which included several saws and axes. He had probably used one of the saws to perform the mutilation.

Ray Pinker examined each of the tools very closely, taking scrapings and subjecting them to chemical tests. Even in the 1940s, the test for the presence of human blood required very little material for a positive result, and one of the saws proved to have human flesh between the teeth. This, together with ballistic evidence, was enough to convict Arthur Eggers.

...veapon

2 The problem when test-firing a suspect weapon is that the bullets must be retrieved in good enough condition so that they can be compared with those fired by the murder weapon. Pinker had a wooden box built, which was filled with densely-packed cotton waste. The gun was fired through the end of the box and the cotton waste stopped the bullets. Pinker then had to search the cotton waste for the used rounds.

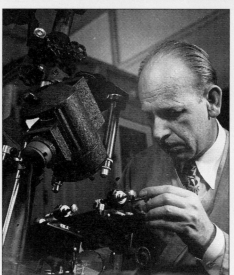

3 After retrieving the bullets, they had to be compared with those recovered from the body of the victim. For this task Pinker used a comparison microscope. This comprises two instruments with a single eyepiece. One bullet is placed in each at the same attitude and viewed under the same magnification. The two images are then superimposed in the single eyepiece, and the examiner can easily see any similarities or differences.

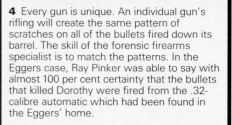

4 Every gun is unique. An individual gun's rifling will create the same pattern of scratches on all of the bullets fired down its barrel. The skill of the forensic firearms specialist is to match the patterns. In the Eggers case, Ray Pinker was able to say with almost 100 per cent certainty that the bullets that killed Dorothy were fired from the .32-calibre automatic which had been found in the Eggers' home.

The Body
under the floorboards

Occasionally the scientific evidence of a Home Office pathologist, called in by police, may actually clear an accused person of a murder charge. Such was the case in the grim affair of Patrick Miller and Barry Stone.

According to people who knew him, 45-year-old labourer and odd-job man Barry Severn Stone was one of the quietest and least offensive of men. "Good as gold," was the verdict of the landlord of the Queen Adelaide pub, where Stone sometimes drank a couple of pints during weekend lunchtimes. "Always polite and pleasant, though he usually sat by himself at a corner table. Never saw him the worse for drink."

Vanished from home

Stone's sister and his former wife agreed. Though Stone had few friends, neither of the women believed him to have

Barry Stone was a quiet man. He was known by sight at his local pub, although he rarely talked much. But when he disappeared in 1983, he was missed. Most people thought he had run off; few could have imagined his gruesome fate.

As a shift worker at local firm Stanton and Stavely, Barry Stone would often not be seen for days. It was, therefore, some time before his neighbours in Devon Street realised that he was missing.

had any enemies. But Nottingham police began to suspect otherwise after Stone suddenly vanished from his home at 31 Devon Street in Nottingham, late in May 1983.

The source of their doubts was Patrick David Miller, a plumber and jobbing builder who lived out of town and occasionally lodged with the missing man when work cropped up in the Nottingham area. Miller, a clean-cut, 46-year-old ex-RAF police-man, appeared reluctant to give his land-lord a bad name, but nevertheless said that, on the quiet, Stone was a "hard-drink-ing womaniser, who was cuter than you think".

Lipstick on the teacups

According to Miller, visitors to Stone's house had from time to time noticed tea-cups smeared with lipstick in the kitchen sink, and women's underclothes hanging on the washing line in his garden. In the absence of any more concrete evidence, the matter was dropped; officially Barry Stone remained on Nottingham police books as a missing person, who may or may not have run off with a mystery blonde woman, perhaps to avoid an avenging hus-band.

A year later, Stone's file was routinely reviewed by Detective Chief Inspector Bruce Foster and Detective Inspector Carl Jackson. They were struck by the fact that Miller was the only one of several wit-nesses to have suggested that Stone had been anything other than ordinary. They also discovered that, since Stone's dis-

Mystery

Barry Stone is missing

Barry Stone vanished in May 1983. A mild-mannered man with no hint of a troubled past, his disappearance was a complete mystery. Divorced and living alone, he had a simple lifestyle. His terraced house in Devon Street was paid for, so he needed little in the way of income for his modest needs, and he survived quite happily on what he could make as a labourer and odd-job man.

Few close friends

Barry Stone had plenty of acquaintances, but few close friends. He would occasionally have a pint or two at the weekend, but could not be said to be a drinker – nobody had ever seen him drunk.

Mysterious disappearance

So why should a man like Barry Stone run away? Could there have been foul play? He might not have had many close friends, but neither did he have any enemies; nobody had a bad word to say about Barry. His disappearance was a total mystery.

"Barry was a womaniser..."

There was one dissenting voice in the picture painted of Barry Stone. Patrick Miller was a former RAF policeman who now worked as an itinerant jobbing builder, and he lodged with Stone whenever he had work in Nottingham. According to Miller, Barry Stone was a lot wilder than he appeared. Miller claimed that Stone was a secret drinker and that he had plenty of intimate women friends.

On one occasion, just before Barry disappeared, Miller's nephew called at the house while Stone was out at work. Although nobody had ever seen a woman in the small terraced house, Miller pointed out women's clothing hanging on the line and lipstick on a glass in the kitchen.

Barry Stone and his occasional lodger, Patrick Miller, were opposites. Miller, an ex-serviceman, was an extrovert keep-fit enthusiast whose passion was cricket.

appearance, a number of reminders from a London-based loan company had arrived at his house. A check revealed that the com-pany's Nottingham agents had loaned Mr Stone £4,000 against the deeds of his house at Devon Street in January 1983 – six months before he had disappeared. More importantly, they found that the signature on the loan agreement forms did not tally with that of Barry Stone.

Miller was again brought in for question-ing, but this time DCI Foster had a shock for him; the agent from the finance com-pany who had arranged the loan with Mr Stone was also present. Though the agent recognised Miller as 'Stone' immediately, the debonair Miller still tried to bluff his way out. "Cool as a cucumber," was Foster's assessment.

In fact by now Miller knew that his game was well and truly up. The following day, when two detective constables called on him in his cell, he asked them: "You know I've done it, lads, don't you?"

After a while he confessed to having taken out the loan in Stone's name. Miller said that Stone had been a party to the fraud, and on the night of 27 May 1983 there had been a fight, during which the ex-military policeman Miller had 'thrown' Stone, who had fallen and hit his head against the floor. He had failed to get up. He was dead.

Miller said that he had then, in panic, wrapped the body in black plastic sheeting and taken it, under the cover of darkness, to an empty house at Wollaton Vale, where he was doing plumbing work for the absent owner. There he had prised up the floor-boards in the lounge, lowered the plastic-shrouded corpse onto the concrete base, and then replaced the floorboards. Then, three months later, in August, when the owner of the house was on holiday, he had

returned and broken through the concrete, buried Stone, and concreted over the grave.

Late in the afternoon of Sunday 3 June 1984, almost before Miller completed his statement, a detachment of police sped out to the well-to-do suburb of Wollaton.

The floorboards were torn up and, sure enough, a tombstone-like slab of hard con-crete lay exposed beneath the harsh police floodlighting, a faint footprint outlined on its otherwise pristine surface. Someone gave the edge of the concrete a tap with a sledgehammer, and the resultant crack re-vealed the dusty shine of black plastic. It was enough; now it was a job for the pathol-ogist.

Body recovered

At 7.30 p.m. Professor Alan Usher, con-sultant Home Office pathologist for the East Midlands area, arrived to begin his examination. Under his supervision, further floorboards were removed and a trench about three feet deep was dug, parallel to the grave. With infinite care the soil under the concrete cap was excavated. Soil samples were removed for later exam-ination. Finally, at around midnight, the

A tomb uncovered

1 Finding the body

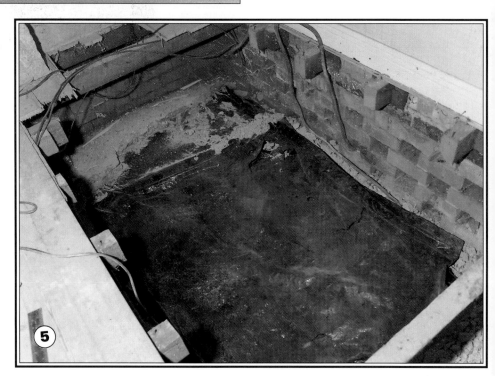

1 Finding the body
As soon as Miller revealed what he had done with Barry Stone's remains, an investigation team, including scene of crime specialists and forensic pathologists, was sent to the house in Wollaton Vale.

2 The precise location
The owner of the house was horrified when he discovered that his front room had been used as a burial site. "I had Miller in to move a radiator and fix some leaking pipes. When the police came and said that they were investigating a serious crime, I was completely shocked. There were so many people investigating that I had to move out."

Patrick Miller admitted that Barry Stone had died at his hands, but said that it had been an accident. He said that he and Stone had used Stone's name and the deeds of his house to fraudulently borrow £4,000.

On 27 May they had argued, and in the fight that followed Miller had pushed Stone, who fell backwards and cracked his skull. Miller said that he wrapped Stone's remains in black plastic sheeting and took them to an empty house where he had been working and dumped the body under the floorboards. He returned three months later when the owner was on holiday and buried the body in the foundations, covering it with concrete.

plastic-covered human shape was lifted out of the grave and into the light.

At 2.30 p.m. on Monday 4 June, Professor Usher began his protracted autopsy at Nottingham District General Hospital. Externally, the body's covering consisted of plastic sheeting wrapped around with knotted electrical cable, which had been formed into a handle at the front so that the bundle could be carried like an elongated cricket bag. Underneath the black plastic covering, the lower legs and feet had been swathed in a fertiliser bag, and the head encased in a plastic carrier bag and a tattered towel. Over these was a second covering consisting of a large green cotton bed cover.

When all these items were removed, the body of a plump man clad in jeans, grey socks, and a badly corroded shirt and jumper was revealed. Because of the combination of the man's obesity and the dampness of the soil with which it had been surrounded, the corpse had undergone the adipocere change, which means that instead of rotting, the head, face, torso, arms and upper legs had changed into a greasy suet, leaving the body looking like a sweaty waxwork. The eyeballs had ▶

5 Layer after layer
In order to expose the body the joists had to be sawn away and the floor was propped up with bricks. After clearing away the concrete, a large sheet of black plastic was revealed, about six feet square, with a body-shaped lump in the middle.

6 Unearthing the body
In order to move the body with as little disturbance as possible, a trench was dug to one side of the remains. A board was then slid underneath and the body was removed.

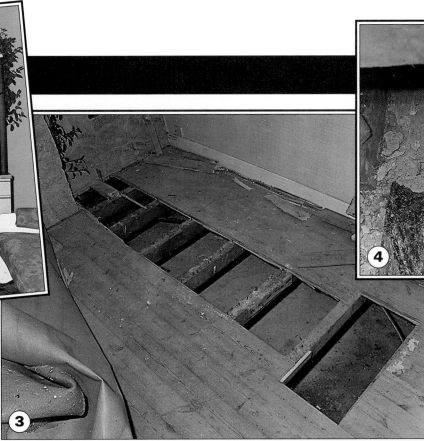

3 Under the carpet
The investigators removed all of the furniture from the living room and pulled up the carpet. The bare floorboards showed that a number had been taken up and replaced. These were removed, to expose a carefully smoothed layer of concrete below.

4 The makeshift tomb
At first, police investigators anticipated great difficulty in retrieving the body from its concrete tomb, assuming there really was a body under the floorboards. But the job was not as hard as they expected. In spite of its solid appearance, the layer of concrete was almost eggshell thin. The excavators found that it could easily be broken up by hammers. Through the concrete rubble, they spotted black plastic.

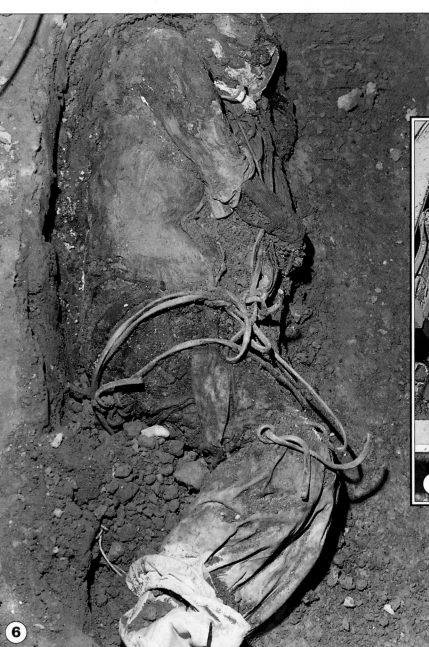

7 Collecting the evidence
Every piece of earth that was removed from the grave was carefully bagged and labelled for further analysis by Cambridge forensic entomologist Dr Zakaria Erzinclioglu. The number and condition of any maggots and fly pupae removed from the site would tell 'Dr Zak' just how long the body had been left before being concreted over.

41

collapsed and gone from the open eyelids, and the ears had been flattened against the head.

Back at Nottingham police headquarters, the investigators had to establish whether death was accidental or premeditated. They decided that Miller's story of Stone having accidentally died during a fight was a fabrication – a ploy used regularly by murderers who had deliberately beaten their victims to death.

The police case

They thought that Miller could not have 'temporarily' dumped the body under the floorboards above the concrete, for the stench of decomposition would have been unbearable during the long hot summer. He must have already prepared the burial site in the concrete slab, and entombed the body into the concrete straight away. For where was the evidence of flies and maggots that surely would have infested the body during those summer months had the body been simply left under the floorboards?

There were airbricks to the outside, and holes around central heating pipes through which flies would have no doubt entered. Doctor Zakaria Erzinclioglu, the eminent forensic entomologist, estimated that

Right: The pitiful remains of Barry Stone are taken from his unsanctified grave. The dampness of the ground in which the body was buried meant that the flesh had largely converted to adipocere, a waxy, suet-like substance.

Right: Scene of crime officers remove material from the house where Stone was buried. Police work is sometimes like an archaeological dig: you have to carefully move an immense amount of material, sifting through it with a fine-tooth comb, looking for the one piece of evidence which will solve the mystery.

Detective Inspector Carl Jackson was one of the officers who charged Patrick Miller.

Detective Chief Inspector Bruce Foster led the inquiry into the disappearance of Barry Stone.

Nottingham people followed the progress of the 'Body under the floor' case from the headlines in the Nottingham Evening Post.

Was the tomb planned?

Much of Patrick Miller's defence rested on whether he had disposed of the body in a spur-of-the-moment panic. The police had grave doubts. Could a corpse have been kept under the floorboards for several weeks in summer without decomposing and stinking to high heaven?

There was also the lack of insect evidence. Flies will generally find a corpse within hours, laying hundreds, if not thousands, of eggs. If Barry Stone's body had been left overnight and then dumped under the floorboards it should have been the target for insect life. Why were there no maggots?

The prosecution case said that the only possibility was that the body had been buried in concrete immediately, which implied premeditation. When it came to trial, however, the jury were not convinced.

Barry Stone's concrete grave bore only one clue – a print of Miller's boot on the surface (left).

there would have been thousands, if not millions, of flies, maggots or pupae cases. But there were none.

The police also concluded that Miller had planted the woman's clothing and marked the cups with lipstick to establish the story of the blonde woman.

Unfortunately, Professor Usher had a disappointment for them. There were no marks of violence on Stone's body apart from a 3 cm long slit in the scalp at the back of the head, and 4 cm crack in the corresponding area of the skull, which had caused bleeding into the tissues surrounding the brain, causing death. Furthermore, the back of Stone's skull was slightly thinner than normal.

Pathologist's report

"I can say," said Professor Usher in his report, "that the degree of putrefaction, given the conditions, was consistent with the time of death given by Miller . . . (and) I can say that the injury I found is consistent with the account of events given by Miller, i.e. Stone having fallen on to the back of his head, either after having been pushed or tripped by Miller, or possibly if the two of them fell with Miller on top of Stone . . . "

Despite this, police pressed a charge of murder, plus further charges of falsely obtaining a loan and unlawfully concealing a body. But they failed to convince the Nottingham High Court jury. Patrick David Miller was found not guilty of murder but was given four years for manslaughter, with concurrent sentences of two-and-a-half years for the fraud and 12 months for concealing the body. □

Evidence

The wound that saved Miller

Miller stated that Stone had fallen backwards during the fight and cracked his head. All too often forensic evidence is used to catch criminals in a lie. But its major function is to establish truth, and in this case it supported the defence. The post-mortem examination of Barry Stone's body revealed no serious injury other than to the back of the skull, which in the view of Professor Alan Usher was consistent with Miller's statement.

Because the body was largely intact, any evidence of violence would have survived to be discovered by the pathologist. Unfortunately for the police case, the crack in the back of the skull was the only significant damage, matching Patrick Miller's statement of accidental injury.

Below: Miller told police that he and Stone had an argument, during the course of which the ex-military policeman had given his landlord a push. Anyone falling backwards will probably hit the ground first with his buttocks, the thick muscular padding preventing injury. The head will then whiplash backwards to strike the floor with stunning force. Unlike other portions of the body the skull has little exterior padding, so this type of impact is very likely to cause serious injury.

Al Packer was one of a party of 20 gold prospectors in the Rocky Mountains. Most turned back with the onset of winter, but Packer and five others went on.

The Colorado
CANNIBAL

In the winter of 1874, six gold prospectors became trapped in the Rocky Mountains. Only Alferd Packer survived – by eating his companions. But did he kill them first?

In a rough, frontier courtroom in Lake City, Colorado, on Friday 13 April 1883, Judge Melville B. Gerry opened the proceedings by pointing ominously at the defendant brought before him for sentencing. Full of righteous fury (and possibly more, for it was after a long and possibly liquid lunchtime), he roared:

"Stand up, y'voracious man-eating son of a bitch, stand up. There was seven Democrats in Hinsdale County and you've ate five of them. God damn you. I sentence you to be hanged by the neck until you is dead, dead, dead, as a warning against reducing the Democrat population of the state. Packer,

you Republican cannibal, I would sentence you to hell but the statutes forbid it."

With that sentence, Alferd G. Packer, the Colorado Cannibal, became not just an unemployed harness maker and failed prospector but claimed his own twisted place in the glorious history of the USA. He did not hang by the neck until he was dead, dead, dead, as Judge Gerry had so fervently and eloquently wished (the transcript shows a much more polished version of the verdict entirely, but in those days such revision was not uncommon). Rather, thanks to legal technicalities, a new trial and a Republican governor sympathetic to

the fact that Packer had, indeed, only eaten Democrats (like Judge Gerry), he ended up walking out of prison on parole after serving 15 years.

Local hero

Today, Alferd Packer's name is still remembered throughout the Great Republic. Institutions as diverse as the National Press Club in Washington DC and the University of Colorado at Boulder have named cafeterias after him. His bust, dedicated by a later Republican governor, is displayed in the Colorado State Capitol. In Lake City, Colorado, he remains the local hero, when all his upstanding and law-abiding contemporaries are long forgotten.

However, no-one was ever sure whether Packer's fame was deserved. He had been convicted of murdering his companions when their prospecting party got lost in the Colorado mountains during the bitterly cold winter of 1874. Packer never denied eating them, nor that, after they were dead, he had 'borrowed' their money and possessions. Since he had been seen in the area looking rather plump after a very lean winter, it would not have done him much good to do so.

But had he killed them first? Cannibalism by itself was not then against the law in Colorado. Packer claimed that all but one of the party had died of natural causes or were killed by another hunger-crazed prospector, Shannon Wilson Bell. Packer claimed that Bell had done this while he was absent from the camp on a fruitless five-day hunting trip and, when Packer returned empty-handed, he found Bell sitting around the camp-fire, roasting the leg of another prospector as an appetiser. The bodies of the other prospectors, with numerous hatchet wounds, lay strewn around, the proof of Bell's earlier crimes.

Bell did not invite Packer to his grisly feast, but instead decided to make him the main course. It was, Packer said, simply self-defence when he shot and killed Bell, who was attacking him, knife (and possibly fork) in hand. Packer, according to his account, then had to stay the winter alone at the campsite, which he did by finishing up the results of Bell's butchering. It was a story neither the jury (nor Judge Gerry) found credible.

While it might not have mattered to the undergraduates wolfing down their 'Packer Snacker' burgers in the Boulder cafeteria, the question of Packer's possible innocence of murder intrigued Professor James Starrs, professor of law and forensics at George Washington University in Washington DC. Always keen to demonstrate the strengths and limitations of modern forensic analysis, Professor Starrs thought an examination of the bones could yield new clues as to what actually happened in the winter of 1874. "From the bones we will be able to see bullet holes and hatch marks from where the skinning knife might have scraped the bones. We'll be able to tell if the victims were cannibalised, if they were struck by a hatchet blow, if they were really near starvation," he said.

The Packer Project

In the summer of 1989, Professor Starrs, having put together 'The Packer Project' with a team of 13 archaeologists, anthropologists, pathologists and technicians, started his search for the bodies of the victims. He was "90 per cent sure" the

Right and below: In 1989 Professor James Starrs decided to uncover the truth behind the Packer story. After finding the massacre site by using old records and publications (inset), a scientific team set about the delicate task of unearthing the remains of Packer's companions: Swan, Miller, Humphrey, Noon and Bell.

Above: When arrested at the Los Pinos Indian Agency, Packer admitted eating his companions, but claimed that they had died of natural causes. However, when a search party found the bodies, near the shores of Lake Christoval, it was clear that they had been hacked and bludgeoned to death.

Cannibal Plateau

Sketch made by John A. Randolph of the victims. From Harper's Weekly, October 17, 1874.

12

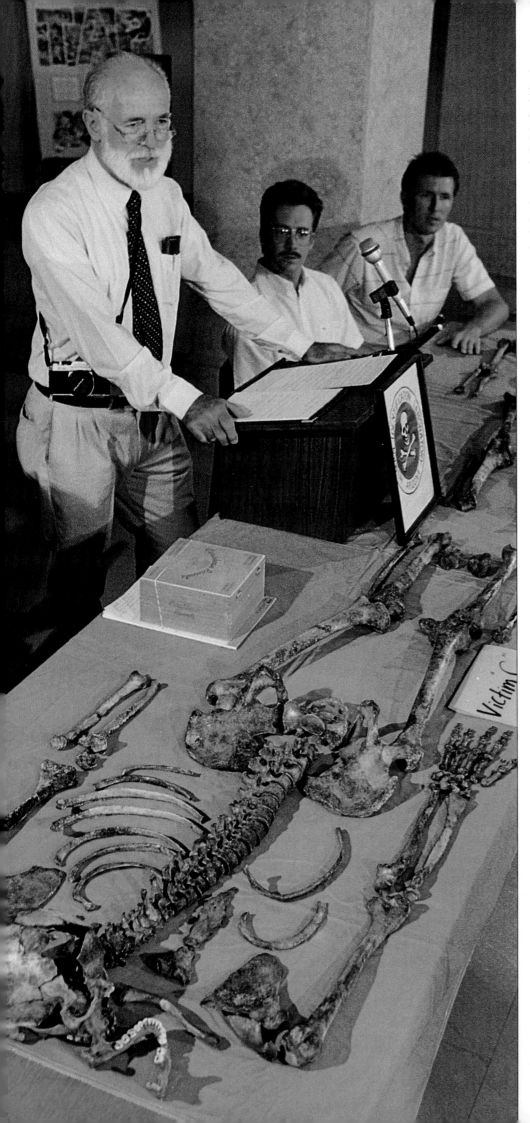

bodies were under a grave marker, put up in 1928, in Deadman's Gulch. The gulch lies between Cannibalism Plateau and Round Top Mountain, about two miles south of Lake City (where, of course, one local diner offers 'The Packer Platter', "for those with a man-sized appetite").

Ground-penetrating radar was used to search for the bodies, which proved to be buried where Professor Starrs thought they were. After exhumation, they were brought to the Arizona State Museum at Tucson for 30 days of analysis.

Left: At a press conference Professor Starrs, showed that the skulls of at least four of the victims had been shattered. Some had been attacked with a hatchet, while 'victim C', seen here, had probably been smashed over the head with a rifle butt.

Right: Al Packer was arrested soon after the events in the mountains, but he escaped from custody. Recognised in Wyoming nine years later, he was again arrested and put on trial for murder. In the century since then argument has raged about Al Packer's guilt or innocence, and his life has become the subject of books and plays.

From the results of this analysis, Professor Starrs reached his own verdict. It was announced in October 1989, though it was not as ringing as Judge Gerry's speech. "Packer was as guilty as sin and his sins were all mortal ones." As for Packer's claim of self-defence: "It is as plain as a pikestaff that Packer was the one who was on the attack, not Bell," Starrs said. The examination of the bones showed that the wounds on the bodies taken from the grave were caused by a hatchet-like instrument at a time when they were defending themselves; marks on the arm bones suggested that the victims had raised their arms to fend off blows, even those who Packer claimed had died of natural causes.

The bones provided clear evidence that at least four of the victims were bludgeoned to death, butcher-style, and then carefully defleshed with a skinning knife. Marks on one bone probably came from a coyote eating the scraps after the spring thaw of 1874, which was consistent with contemporary reports that what was left of the bodies was incomplete and possibly scattered by animals. There was no evidence that any had suffered gunshot wounds.

However, there were limits to the evidence that could be drawn from the bones. Professor Starrs admitted he could not be sure which set of bones were that of Bell, and could not make sure that the blows right scenario, but scientifically we cannot substantiate it." Birkby added that while the evidence showed that the victims had indeed been murdered and cannibalised, there was no evidence to suggest who had done it, other than the fact that the wounds were inconsistent with Packer's testimony. "We'll never know who did it based on any solid physical evidence. We're never going to know."

But even after the bones were re-interred in a single coffin under the grave marker in Deadman's Gulch, Professor Starrs remained convinced. "This latest evidence convicts him [Packer] beyond a shadow of a doubt. Packer was having his flesh fillets morning, noon and night, even though he could have lived by killing rabbits. Packer was a fiend, base, brutish . . . barbaric."

Examining the bones in detail proved that the prospectors had been murdered, then defleshed by a skinning knife. The evidence strongly implies that Al Packer was indeed a vicious cannibal killer.

seen on the bodies were administered by Packer and not Bell. Part of the reason for the problems was that not only were the skeletons not all complete, but there were limited physical descriptions of the men available to compare the bones with. This meant that even if the scientists had been able to determine whether the wounds were inflicted by cutting left-handed or right-handed from the angle of the marks on the bone, they could not know who in the ill-fated party was left- and right-handed. The height of each man – which could have provided clues if marks on the bones were to show upwards or downwards strokes – was also largely unknown.

Who was the murderer?

Physical anthropologist Walter H. Birkby of the Arizona State Museum, who had carried out the 26-day analysis of the bones, added further caveats. He thought that Starrs' version – of mass slaughter by Packer – was consistent with the evidence. But, Birkby said: "It could possibly be the

POISON PELLET MURDER

Above: Todor Zhivkhov was a hard-line Communist whose rule in Bulgaria was continually challenged by exiles like Georgi Markov.

Right: Markov was a talented writer who regularly broadcast satirical digs at the Communist establishment via the BBC World Service.

The murder of Bulgarian exile Georgi Markov brought the world of Cold War espionage to the streets of London.

Georgieu Ivanov Markov was a 49-year-old Bulgarian playwright, novelist and avowed anti-Communist who had defected to the West in 1969, arriving in England in 1971. Since that time he had been employed by the BBC World Service to broadcast on cultural and political matters to his native Bulgaria. His broadcasts were carried not only by the

BBC but also by Deutsche Welle in Cologne and the CIA-sponsored Radio Free Europe in Munich.

Markov's weekly broadcasts were never overtly anti-Communist but they were distinctly satirical, and he did little to disguise his loathing for the political regime in his homeland. Over the years his broadcasts made him some powerful enemies

among the Bulgarian hierarchy.

On Thursday 7 September 1978, Markov was due to work an evening shift at the BBC studios at Bush House in Aldwych. At about 2.30 p.m., he drove from his home in Clapham and, because of parking restrictions in central London at that time of day, he left his Simca on a meter on the South Bank and walked the remaining three-

Rush-hour accident?

It appeared to have been one of those little accidents which happen all the time during the rush hour in a crowded city. While passing a bus stop near London's Waterloo Bridge, Georgi Markov had been spiked by a man with an umbrella. Curiously, the umbrella seemed to have pierced the skin. A small, livid mark was left on the back of Markov's thigh where it had made contact, which he pointed out to a colleague at the BBC and to his wife when he got home later that evening.

quarters of a mile over Waterloo Bridge to work.

At 6.30 p.m., as was his habit every couple of hours, he left Bush House to feed the meter where his car was parked. En route to the South Bank he walked past a crowded bus stop. Suddenly he felt a stinging sensation in the back of his right thigh. He turned around and saw a man brandishing an umbrella. The man, apparently responsible for prodding Markov, apologised in a thick foreign accent. He then flagged down a cab, climbed in, and disappeared into the rush-hour traffic before Markov had a chance to challenge him.

Umbrella incident

Markov returned to his office and told a colleague, Teo Lirkoff, about the incident. Lirkoff noticed a spot of blood on the back of Markov's jeans. Markov dropped his trousers and Lirkoff pointed out an angry red spot on the back of his friend's leg. Markov was satisfied that the whole episode had been an accident, and decided to get on with his work. He did a few trans-

lations, read the 9.30 news and returned to his home in Clapham at about 10.30 p.m. He told his wife, Annabel, about his run-in with the brolly-wielding foreigner and showed her his 'wound', but neither of them viewed the matter very seriously.

The following morning, however, Markov woke with a high fever and started to vomit. His throat felt tight and he had difficulty speaking. A few hours later he was admitted to St James's Hospital in nearby Balham. There he was examined by Dr Bernard Riley and was found to have a rapid pulse and swollen lymph glands. Annabel Markov was beginning to suspect that there was a connection between her husband's sudden illness and the incident at the bus stop. She told doctors what had happened, but the medical fraternity were not overly impressed by stories of Bulgarian secret agents and poisoned umbrellas. They did, however, X-ray Markov's thigh, but the film showed nothing abnormal.

Markov's condition continued to deteriorate rapidly and later that morning he was transferred to intensive care. His blood pressure plummeted while his pulse

soared to 160 beats per minute, double its normal rate; his body temperature dropped and he was incapable of urinating, a condition that indicated kidney failure. He vomited constantly and there were traces of blood in his vomit. Tests showed that his white cell count was three times its normal level.

The attending physicians were baffled by Markov's symptoms, but suspected that he was probably suffering from septicaemia. Early on the morning of Sunday 11 September, Markov's condition had become critical. An electrocardiograph showed that there was a blockage to the conductive system of his heart and surgeons prepared to introduce a pacemaker. Before the operation could be performed, however, Markov went into a delirious state and ripped out all his intravenous drips. The shock to his system was colossal and, at 9.45 a.m., his heart stopped. Doctors spent an hour trying to resuscitate him, but it was hopeless and, at 10.40 a.m., Georgi Markov was pronounced dead.

Poisoned

The following day an autopsy was performed on Markov's body by forensic pathologist Dr Rufus Crompton. Examination of the lungs, liver, intestines, lymph glands, testicles and pancreas all pointed to the fact that Georgi Markov had been poisoned.

Crompton was aware of Annabel Markov's theory that her husband had been the victim of an attack by enemy agents, and while he later admitted that he was highly sceptical, he did take the precaution of cutting away a section of flesh from around the wound, and a corresponding section from the other thigh. He sealed these samples in plastic bags and sent them over to the Metropolitan Police Forensic Laboratory at Lambeth.

While the medical profession were not taking the assassination theory seriously, the police certainly were. A full-scale investigation into Markov's death was immediately launched, headed by Commander James Nevill of Scotland Yard's Anti-Terrorist Squad. On his orders, the tissue samples taken from Markov's legs were sent for examination by the govern-

The Sun
12 September 1978

'POISON BROLLY MURDER' RIDDLE

Yard probe 'street attack' on defector

By ROBERT TRAINI

A DEFECTOR from Communism who died mysteriously in London yesterday may have been murdered—with a poisoned umbrella tip.

This amazing theory was being probed by Scotland Yard detectives last night.

The man, 49-year-old Georgi Ivanov Markov, was a broadcaster for the BBC's overseas service. He was opposed to Communism and is said to have made many enemies.

An incident occurred on Thursday as he was standing in a bus queue near Bush House, Aldwych, after leaving the BBC studios there. He told friends he was in collision with a man who appeared to be running to get a taxi.

The point of the man's umbrella struck Mr Markov in the right thigh. The man then dropped the umbrella, picked it up and disappeared.

Mr Markov had a minor thigh injury — caused, he believed, by poison in the umbrella tip.

SHE IS THE ONE ... WANTS

Above: Georgi Markov's wife and friends soon associated his sudden illness with the unusual encounter on Waterloo Bridge. It seemed ridiculous, but could the umbrella tip have been poisoned? Was Georgi the victim of a politically-inspired attack?

Above: Annabel Markov, together with Georgi's brother Nikola and the rest of the family, saw the collapse of Communism as a chance to find out who had murdered her husband. Clearly it had been the work of the Bulgarian Secret Police, but who had ordered the assassination?

Police took the theory that Markov had been assassinated very seriously, particularly when they received news that another Bulgarian exile had undergone a similar attack in Paris.

ment's top-secret chemical defence establishment at Porton Down in Wiltshire.

At Porton Down the investigation was put in the hands of pathologist Dr David Gall, one of the country's leading experts on poisons and nerve agents. By his own admission Gall almost missed the one clue to the cause of Markov's death.

Mystery object

While examining the tissue from the right thigh, he said he saw "that Rufus [Crompton] had put a pin in to keep his orientation and had pushed it in to the hilt to give him some sort of mark. Idly, as one does, I just tipped this with my gloved finger to make sure that was what it was. To my alarm the 'pin head' moved an inch across the tissue. It was a loose piece of metal. It was really very lucky that it did not roll off the post-mortem table on to the floor, under the cupboard and down the drain."

Gall examined the object, which measured less than 1.5 mm in diameter. To the naked eye it appeared to be a simple metal bead, but under a microscope it turned out to be a pellet, which had been drilled with two tiny holes at right angles to one another. "Through one I could see daylight," Gall said, "through the other I could see nothing as there was clearly a lot of congealed tissue inside." Gall sent the pellet back to the police laboratory for detailed examination while he and his team got on with the job of identifying the poison that had killed Markov.

They could find no trace of poison in the body and so they were forced to work backwards from Markov's symptoms. They quickly eliminated bacterial and viral infections, along with diphtheria and tetanus toxins. Endotoxin, which would have accounted for Markov's high blood pressure and elevated white cell count, was also dismissed because of the quantity that would have been needed for it to prove lethal. Most chemical poisons were similarly dismissed. Soon Gall and his colleagues were forced to conclude that they were dealing with some form of organic poison, a toxin produced naturally by a plant or animal.

One by one these too were eliminated, either because the symptoms they produced were inconsistent with those shown by Georgi Markov, or for practical considerations. In the end, they could find only one substance that matched all the conditions – ricin.

Lethal substance

Ricin is a derivative of the castor bean, a lethal substance roughly 500 times as toxic by weight as cyanide or arsenic. The Porton Down scientists knew a bit about ricin, but not enough. In the past they had conducted experiments on small animals, and the symptoms recorded were remarkably similar to those demonstrated by Markov – starting with fever and a high white blood cell count, moving on to shock, lymph node and kidney damage, and ending with haemorrhaging and death.

To be sure that ricin was in fact the culprit, Dr Frank Beswick of Porton Down's medical division decided to conduct an experiment on a pig – an animal of equivalent bulk and similar anatomical structure to man. The animal was injected with a minute quantity of the poison. Six hours later, it developed a fever and its white cell count started to rise. The following day, the unfortunate beast developed cardiac arrhythmia and, 24 hours after the injection, it died. A post-mortem on the pig revealed almost identical internal damage to that found in the body of Georgi Markov.

At the police forensic laboratories, meanwhile, the metal pellet that had been found embedded in Markov's leg was being scrutinised. It was analysed under a scanning electron microscope and was found to be composed of an alloy of 90 per cent platinum and 10 per cent iridium, an alloy harder than steel and impervious to corrosion. The two holes in the pellet, which measured less than .35 mm in diameter, had either been drilled into the material or created by spark erosion. While hardly high-tech, a degree of craftsmanship had been employed in producing the pellet, an object that had clearly been designed for a specific purpose, presumably that of introducing a minute but lethal dose of ricin into the bloodstream of Georgi Markov. The platinum/iridium alloy was sufficiently hard to avoid distortion while passing through the victim's clothing. The material

Right: Georgi Markov worked mainly at the BBC World Service in Bush House in central London, but it was his broadcasts over Radio Free Europe in Munich which made him a thorn in the side of the repressive Communist regime in Sofia.

Below: The assassination of Markov on the streets of London in broad daylight caused a public outcry. But the identity of the actual assassin was never discovered.

was also biologically inert so that it was unlikely to be rejected by the body or detected by causing wide-spread inflammation, and it had the added advantage of being radio-opaque so that it would be almost invisible on an X-ray.

When Markov's X-rays were re-examined, the pellet could in fact just be detected in the shadow of the femur, but it was so small and so vague that it had been mistaken for a speck of dust on the photographic plate.

Unanswered questions

The facts were falling into place. The police were now convinced that Markov had been deliberately killed by a pellet that had carried a lethal cargo of approximately 0.2 milligrams of ricin. Two questions remained unanswered. How had the pellet been introduced into Markov's body? And who had done it?

At first police examined the possibility that the pellet had been jabbed into the victim's leg with the point of the much-publicised umbrella, but practical tests proved that this would have been extremely difficult. They also discounted the possibility that a conventional firearm had been used. Even with a silencer, the report would have been considerable – Markov heard nothing – and, fired at close range, the shot

Enemy of the state

Georgieu Ivanov Markov was born in Sofia in 1929, the son of a Bulgarian army officer. He qualified as a chemical engineer and spent several years in industry before becoming a professional writer. His first work, two volumes of short stories, was published in 1961. His fame in Bulgaria grew and he soon found himself mixing with the elite of Sofia, including Todor Zhivkhov and other leading members of the Bulgarian Communist Party.

Markov defects

Markov himself was no lover of the Communist regime and his work became increasingly critical of life in the Soviet bloc in general and Bulgaria in particular. By 1969, the elite of Sofia no longer lionised Georgie Markov, but saw him as an enemy of the state. The situation was becoming intolerable, and in June of that year Markov defected while on a visit to Italy. This defection, together with a collectin of his essays entitled "Meetings with Todor Zhivkhov", made him a non-person in Bulgaria, as well as a target for assassination.

Broadcasting job

In 1971 Markov left Italy and settled in London, where he accepted a post as a broadcaster with the BBC World Service. He enjoyed his adopted home and settled into suburban life with his English wife Annabel and their daughter, Sasha. His first book since leaving Bulgaria, *The Right Honourable Chimpanzee*, was completed a few weeks before his death, and was published shortly afterwards.

Castor bean killer

Ricin, the substance that killed Georgi Markov, is an extremely toxic protein derived from the castor bean (*Ricinus communis*). It causes a slow and painful death, generally over a period of about 48 hours, during which time the victim will suffer from fever, a high white blood cell count, shock, damage to the kidneys and lymph nodes, and massive and widespread haemorrhaging.

Ricin is lethal in minute doses. It is estimated that no more than 0.2 milligrams was contained in the pellet fired into Markov's thigh. Markov weighed about 11 stone and it would have taken approximately 100 milligrams of arsenic or cyanide to have the same devastating effect.

Attempted suicide

The castor beans from which ricin is derived are poisonous in their own right, but only in very large quantities. In 1982, a report issued by the Mid America Poison Centre described a suicide attempt by the ingestion of castor beans. A man called the centre to say that, after extensive research, he had

decided to end his own life by ricin poisoning and that he had swallowed more than 50 castor beans. The caller was extremely annoyed that so far they had had no effect. The telephone call was traced and an ambulance was despatched to pick the man up.

He was rushed to hospital and his stomach was pumped, recovering several partly

digested castor beans, and he was given activated charcoal as a binding agent. Some hours later, he developed severe stomach pains and showed signs of kidney failure; his pulse rate increased and his blood pressure dropped dramatically. After being rehydrated intravenously, however, his condition improved, and after four days he was discharged from hospital.

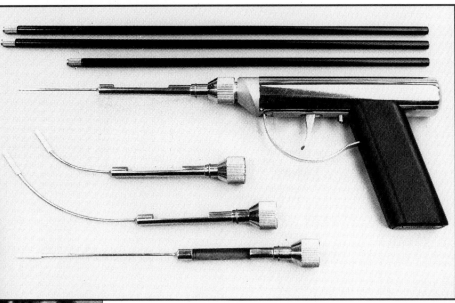

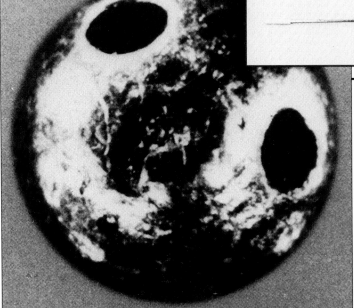

Above: The gas gun used to inject the poison pellet was probably acquired by the Bulgarians from the Soviet KGB. Once fitted with extension tubes, the gun could be fired through an umbrella.

Left: The deadly platinum/iridium pellet was just over a millimetre in diameter, and contained about 0.2 milligrams of poison.

would have left powder burns on Markov's jeans – forensic examination of his clothing revealed no such burns. In fact, it was hard to detect the spot where the pellet had passed through the fabric, which suggested that it must have travelled at some considerable speed. It was also unlikely that a needle had been used to introduce the pellet, because the diameter of the needle required would have been such as to cause Markov excruciating pain, rather than the sharp stinging sensation he had described. Forensic scientists could come up with only one sensible explanation: that the pellet had been propelled by some form of high-powered gas or compressed-air gun that had been incorporated into the umbrella.

As to who had been responsible for the

killing, the police and MI5 were in little doubt that it was the work of the Bulgarian Secret Service. The USSR were the world's leading manufacturers of platinum/iridium alloys, and ricin was the subject of intensive research in Hungary. So it was fairly obvious that, not only had the Bulgarians been responsible for the assassination, they had carried it out with the knowledge and approval of their Soviet masters.

Killing denied

Knowing that the Bulgarian Secret Service had been responsible for the death of Georgi Markov and proving it were two totally different matters, however. Diplomats at the Bulgarian Embassy in London were confronted, but they denied any

knowledge of the affair, describing allegations that their secret police had been somehow involved as "absurd".

Who was the assassin?

Despite strenuous police efforts, the man with the umbrella was never found and, hamstrung by diplomatic immunity, the police effectively closed the case. One person, however, was not prepared to let the matter rest. Mrs Annabel Markov, Georgi's widow, hoped for the next 12 years for a public enquiry into her husband's death. In was not until 1991 and the collapse of Communism, however, that these hopes were partially fulfilled. Reluctantly and guardedly, the new government admitted that their predecessors had sanctioned several assassinations of Bulgarian defectors, among them Georgieu Ivanov Markov. They promised an enquiry, and then retracted the promise. Attempts by both Mrs Markov and the British authorities to persuade the Bulgarian government to identify the individual responsible and present him for trial, have so far been strenuously resisted. □

Above: Millions of people suffered and died under the iron rule of Marxism. Georgi Markov was one. The new Bulgarian government has been slow to rehabilitate Markov – his writings have now been published in Sofia, but Georgi remains a non-person.

Mystery

Secret police in London

Despite the public outcry at the murder of Georgi Markov and the attempt on the life of his friend, Vladimir Kostov, the Bulgarian Secret Service was not deterred from its goal of silencing dissidents. Four days after Markov's death, General Dimiter Stoyanov, the minister for internal affairs and head of the secret police, appeared on Bulgarian television and made this horrifying statement: "Our enemies cannot evade our action anywhere," he boasted, "For us, borders do not exist."

Colleague found dead

Three weeks later, another Bulgarian employee of the BBC, Vladimir Simeonov, was found dead in suspicious circumstances. Simeonov, a 30-year-old translator, died from inhaling blood after falling down the stairs of his home in east London. His injuries, which included a broken nose and a split lip, were described by a pathologist as "unusual" in this type of accident. A post-mortem revealed no trace of alcohol or drugs in the victim's body, and no medical condition that would have explained the fall.

Insufficient evidence

Added to this, Simeonov had been in contact with Commander James Nevill a few days before his accident, after he had received threats from a Bulgarian seaman in the foyer of the BBC. While Nevill and his colleagues were certain that Simeonov had been yet another victim of assassination, they had insufficient evidence, and the inquest returned a verdict of accidental death.

In spite of, or possibly because of, acts like the murder of Georgi Markov, Todor Zhivkhov (third from right in this meeting of Communist leaders in the late 1980s) was ousted from power in Bulgaria.

The Exploded Body

The violent death of gangster Randy Bethell was to pose crime investigators a major identification problem.

The streets and waterways of Miami are glamorous, but since the 1970s they have also been the site of a violent drugs war. Randy Bethell was a minor player in the game, whose death was to lead to the breaking of a major drugs gang.

It was 7.30 in the evening of 4 September 1975. A police car drew up next to utility pole number 136 on Card Sound Road in Monroe County, near Miami. The police had been looking for members of the Cravero gang for months, and they'd had a tip-off that the body of one of them was here.

It didn't take the searchers long to find something in the wooded area at the side of the road. But it was not a body. Not intact, at least. What they saw was a four-foot crater in the ground, with fragments of bone and clothing scattered in every direction.

The story had started some years previously. Modern-day Florida has always been a pretty violent place. Smuggling is rife, with access to myriad islands of the Bahamas only a short boat or plane trip away. Beyond the Bahamas lie the diverse and often poorly policed islands of the Caribbean, and only another step further is

the mainland of South America.

In the 1970s the American drug problem was just beginning to spread from specialised groups into the mainstream of society. Drugs like marijuana, cocaine and heroin were being smuggled in ever-increasing quantities, much of it through Florida, and illicit fortunes were being made.

The Cravero gang

One organisation that specialised in the importation of cocaine was controlled by gang boss Richard Douglas Cravero. Cravero was a violent man, who had a fatally abrupt way of dealing with competitors and was scarcely less brutal with erring members of his own gang.

The Cravero gang's drug interests were enough to place them on the FBI's surveillance list. The law was on their trail when rumours began circulating that a gang member had been 'executed'. Creighton Randall 'Randy' Bethell had not been seen since 19 February 1975. But nobody could be made to talk about what had happened.

Nobody would talk, that is, until Cravero and 17 members of his gang were arrested later that year on drug charges. Four of them, including Cravero, were also charged with the murder of Stanley Harris, a disaffected member of the gang who had been gunned down outside a North Dade bar early in 1974. With Cravero safely locked up, eyewitnesses were willing to come forwards and make statements, and

Who was he?

It took a great deal of imagination to recognise the remains found near Card Sound Road as a man. Five sticks of dynamite can make a pretty comprehensive mess of a human body, and putting a name to the remains seemed an impossible task.

The investigators had to carry out a painstaking, inch-by-inch search, collecting the scattered fragments of bone in the hope that something would be found that could be identified.

Metropolitan Dade County

OFFICE OF THE MEDICAL EXAMINER

1700 N. W. 10th Avenue

Miami, Florida 33136

SEE 79-1331

UNKNOWN REMAINS

NAME OF DECEASED ___Creighton R. Bethel___ (TENTATIVE)   CASE NO. ___2047___ A

ADDRESS ___2636 N.E. 205th Street, Rural, Fla.___ AGE __28__ RACE White SEX Male

PLACE OF DEATH ___POLE#136-Card Sound Road, (S.R.905), Monroe County, Fla.___

TIME AND DATE DEATH: FOUND _7:30PM:9/4/75_
OCCURRED ___
PRONOUNCED ___ MED. INVESTIGATOR ___

INVESTIGATING AGENCY ___PSD#197221 T Homicide___
(PE)   POLICE INVESTIGATOR __Dt.Felton__

HISTORY Deceased was abducted from Hollywood on 2/19/75, and taken alive to Card Sound Road, Monroe County, Fla. At that location, deceased was allegedly shot in the head with a .357 Magnum revolver. Body was left for a short time and on subsequent trips ;by assailants, the following events followed: 1 trip the teeth were knocked out and jaw removed and disposed of:2nd.trip, the assailants found out that deceased had pins in his knees, an injury from Army, so assailants the shot gunned his knees to prevent identification;3rd.trip-assailants placed a five stick of dynamite bomb on the deceased and detonated it with a timing device;4th.trip- was to observe the area & being happy with the results,felt confident that no remains could be identified. On 9/4/75, Monroe County Sheriff police found remains of deceased scattered in general area of Pole#136,Card Sound Road,Monroe County. Shirt &wig from deceased were identified by the father of the deceased at Medical Examiners Office.

Date and time : Feb. 19,1975, Abt. 10:00 p.m.

Location of incident: Near Card Sound Road, Monroe Co. Fla.

PRIMARY CAUSE OF DEATH ___Gunshot wound of head___

DUE TO: ___

DUE TO: ___

CONT. CAUSE OF DEATH ___

TOXICOLOGICAL FINDINGS ___

PROBABLE MANNER OF DEATH ___Homicide___

AUTOPSY / EXAMINED ___ ONSET OF TERMINAL EVENT: _Field_

FUNERAL DIRECTOR ___Florida Mortuary___ (DATE) BY __Elidio Fernandez/ Joseph H. Davis,M.D.__

REMOVED BY ___

DATE ___ TIME ___

118.01—9   (OVER)

Randy Bethell's fate came to light.

Bethell had got into trouble with Cravero for holding back on some of the take on drug deals. He was abducted from a friend's house in Hollywood on 19 February 1975. At about 10 p.m. Cravero and a group of accomplices took Bethell to Card Sound Road, Monroe County. There the prisoner was shot in the head with a .357 Magnum revolver and was left, with the killers

Above: Following a tip-off, police from Monroe County, north of Miami, went to a spot on Card Sound Road where they expected to find a body. What they found was a crater, four feet across. A careful search produced most of a human body, and the location of each piece was carefully mapped (top) in the medical examiner's report.

Left: The remains were taken to the Dade County Medical Examiner's Office for analysis. They discovered that the victim had not only been blown up: a systematic attempt to destroy any forensic clues to his identity had been carried out by the killers. The skull was shattered and the jaws and teeth had been ripped out. The victim's knees had also been blasted with a shotgun, as they had been surgically pinned and could therefore have provided a clue to his identity. Enough of the skull remained, however, to show part of an entry wound caused by a bullet from a powerful handgun, probably a .357 Magnum.

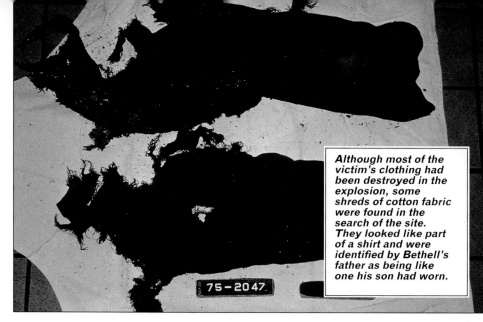

Although most of the victim's clothing had been destroyed in the explosion, some shreds of cotton fabric were found in the search of the site. They looked like part of a shirt and were identified by Bethell's father as being like one his son had worn.

believing that the body would not be found in such a remote wooded location.

Apparently they must have changed their minds, because they returned to the body several times and systematically tried to remove all evidence that could possibly be used in identification. In the first trip, most of the body's teeth and jaws were knocked out and disposed of, using a large boulder to smash the skull. Later the killers discovered that Bethell had been involved in an accident during his army days and he'd had both knees pinned, which would appear on the victim's medical record. So they went back to the body and blasted the knees with a shotgun.

Finally, the gang decided to make the remains completely unidentifiable, once and for all. They blew the body to pieces with a bomb made from five sticks of dynamite. This, they obviously thought, would do the trick, since if the authorities lacked an identifiable body they would find it hard to prove murder.

Identifying the remains

Now that the police had found the remains, they had to prove that this scattered and incomplete skeleton was Randy Bethell. If they did so, it would corroborate the testimony of witnesses and would make another plank in the State and Federal case against the Cravero gang.

A painstaking search of the area around the bomb crater turned up a surprising amount of human debris, as well as shreds of clothing. Enough of the victim's shirt had survived to be identified by Bethell's father, and he also recognised his son's

wig. However, it was the bodily remains that were to prove the clincher.

Back at the Dade County Medical Examiner's office, examination of a large fragment of skull revealed evidence of the passage of a large-calibre bullet. That part of the witnesses' story seemed to be true. But without the teeth, how could anybody conclusively identify the remains? Fortune favoured the investigators, however, when a large fragment of the lower right jaw still holding three teeth was found.

Examination of the bone showed that one of the teeth had been filled and another had undergone more extensive rebuilding with a large silver filling. An X-ray examination showed that the silver filling had been held in place with two pins. Next to it there was evidence of an old extraction.

Now all that was required was the victim's dental record to compare it with this jaw. Fortunately for the investigators, like

many Americans of his generation Bethell had served a stint in the army. His records were tracked down fairly quickly and were passed to Richard R. Souviron, Associate Medical Examiner of Dade County and one of Florida's most experienced forensic odontologists.

Souviron noted that according to Bethell's record he'd had a bicuspid removed in 1967. The healing of the space on the jaw found on Card Sound Road was consistent with an extraction seven years previously. Tooth number 31 on the dental records, a molar, had been filled just as the same tooth on the victim had been filled. Finally, and most tellingly, tooth number 30 had been reconstructed and had been held in place by two pins. Souviron had no doubts. The remains found on Card Sound Road had indeed once been Creighton Randall Bethell, and the case against the Cravero gang was solid. □

Proof of identity

Proving the identity of a corpse can be difficult enough without the murderers having blown it to pieces. In such circumstances a totally unknown body might remain unidentified, since there will often be no clues at all.

However, in the case of the shattered skeleton found in Card Sound Road, the investigators already had a possible name. All they had to do was to prove it.

In the absence of a recognisable face or fingerprints, the best method of identification is forensic dentistry, where the teeth of the victim are matched with pre-death dental records. The problem was finding the teeth, since the killers had taken great pains to mutilate any identifiable portion of the corpse.

Right: Although the killers tried to destroy all dental evidence, by a stroke of good fortune the search of the crime scene turned up a small piece of jawbone still containing three teeth.

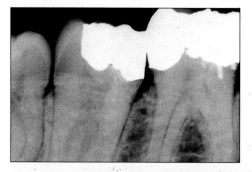

Left: An X-ray examination of the three surviving teeth showed that they had undergone extensive dental work at some time in the past. If the police could match these to Randy Bethell's dental chart, then the victim's identity could be confirmed.

Right: The three teeth were from the right lower jaw, numbers 30, 31 and 32 in the American standard dental designation. Bethell's dental records (top) showed extensive work on teeth 30 and 31. Doctor Souviron's charting of the teeth from the body (below) showed the same work.

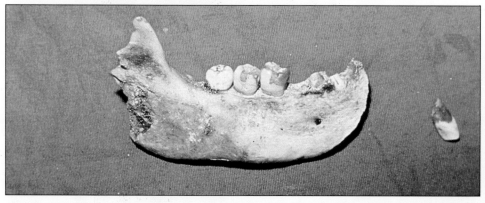

The Cravero gang

THE MIAMI HERALD Wed., March 16, 1977

4-B BRO

Dade Officials Seek Return of Suspect In Bombing of Nightclub Owner's Car

By JOE CRANKSHAW
Herald Staff Writer

Paul (Jake the Snake) Jacobson, who slipped out of the Dade County Jail in January 1976 because of a jailer's error, is being held for Miami authorities in a Los Angeles jail under $500,000 bond.

Jacobson, 30, reportedly a member of the old Rick Cravero gang which was broken up by police with the arrest and conviction of Cravero, was arrested Friday night by the FBI on a charge of unlawful flight to avoid prosecution.

Jacobson is charged with the October 1974 bombing of the car of Miami nightclub owner Stuart Goldman, and with being an accessory to the 1975 murder of Creighton Randall Bethel in Monroe County.

U.S. Magistrate Harvey A. Schneider set March 23 as the date by which authorities must produce the charges and prove that Jacobson is the man they are seeking.

IF THE government prevails at the hearing, Jacobson will be handed over to the Los Angeles County Sheriff's Department for extradition to Miami, said Thomas Kontos, Jacobson's court-appointed attorney.

Ralph Page, Metro Dade Public

to extradite Jacobson if he refuses to return voluntarily.

Jacobson was charged with planting the bomb which resulted in Goldman, owner of the Climax and Pieces of Eight lounges, losing both legs below the knees, two fingers and one eye.

Goldman was sitting in his Cadillac outside his townhouse, 13524 NE 23rd Pl., when the blast took place.

After 18 months of investigation, police arrested Jacobson in the Four O'Clock Club in Hollywood and placed him in the Dade County Jail until he could be indicted.

Jacobson was ordered held without bond, but Corrections Officer John Ripple mistakenly wrote on Jacobson's prison card that he was eligible for release on a $3,500 bond.

INVESTIGATORS also learned that two suspicious telephone calls figured in Jacobson's escape a year ago.

A call was placed to jailers from a man pretending to be Metro De-

tective Tom Stone instructing them to release Jacobson at once. The jailers refused.

But shortly afterward, a U.S. marshal, who had received what he thought was a phone call from an assistant U.S. attorney, appeared at the Dade jail and announced that federal charges of unlawful flight to avoid prosecution had been dropped.

Since flight charges are routinely dropped after state charges are instituted, the jailers released Jacobson.

WHEN FBI agents on Friday arrested Jacobson, whom they had been keeping under surveillance, he was using the name Larry L.

Baker, according to FBI spokesmen. He was unarmed and driving a car in the San Fernando Valley area.

Jacobson was one of 17 members of the Cravero gang arrested on federal charges of operating a $200-million cocaine ring in 1974.

In July 1975, Jacobson was acquitted of the 1974 machinegun slaying of Stanley Harris, said to be a disaffected Cravero gang member. Cravero and two others were convicted of the killing which took place on Valentine's Day 1974.

Jacobson will face the bombing charges in Dade Circuit Court and the murder charges in Monroe County if he is returned to Miami.

JACOBSON

Richard Cravero was sentenced to three life terms. He hit the headlines in 1987 when he escaped from prison, but he was recaptured a couple of days later.

Richard Cravero was a Florida gang leader with Mafia connections. His activities in the burgeoning drug trade in Florida in the 1970s had put him at the head of the FBI's most wanted list, but his ruthless elimination of opponents — his gang was credited with as many as 35 killings — made people afraid to testify against him. It was not until he and 17 of his gang members were arrested that witnesses were persuaded to talk. Among other things, it was the slaughter of Randy Bethell which was to lead to his downfall.

Flaming Murder

The fatal fire was an accident – or so everybody thought. But the victim in the garage had not died in an accident. He had been murdered. It was an almost perfect crime.

The comfortable house on Miami's SW 138 Street had a large garage attached. Inside, Lebanese-born Ezzat Aboul-Hosn (inset) liked to tinker with old cars. When the garage burned, it seemed clear to fire investigators that Aboul-Hosn had burned with it underneath his Chevrolet Vega.

It was just after nine, on a warm Miami evening in May. At her house on SW 138 Street, Mrs James Kell heard an explosion. Looking out of the window, she saw black smoke billowing from behind the closed doors of a garage across the street. It belonged to a ranch-style three-bedroomed house that had been rented some months previously by a Lebanese man called Ezzat Aboul-Hosn.

Mrs Kell telephoned the fire brigade immediately, while her husband and a passing jogger ran across to the scene of the fire. Putting their ears to the door of the garage, they thought they could hear feeble cries. Within minutes, the street was full of firefighters. They were joined by Bassam Wakil, a wealthy Syrian friend of Aboul-Hosn, who had to be forcibly restrained from running into the blazing garage in search of his friend.

When the flames were extinguished a charred body was found pinned under the 1972 Chevrolet Vega in the gutted garage. The car had to be jacked up to free it. The body's fists were clenched, with the limbs drawn up in the 'pugilistic' attitude of the typical fire victim.

"Even if I had known him, I wouldn't have been able to identify him," said Fire Lieutenant Pratt. "I believe he was alive at the time of the fire."

Sequence of events

The sequence of events pieced together by the investigators seemed pretty clear. At 5.30 on the afternoon of the fire, Aboul-Hosn had crossed the street to borrow a pair of pliers from his neighbour, James Kell. He said that he was working on the faulty fuel line of his Chevrolet Vega. It was perhaps a little odd that a man who had declared that his hobby was tinkering with old cars should have to borrow a pair of pliers, but it was not enough to comment on.

Soon afterwards, according to the report submitted by the investigating officers, Bassam Wakil called and found his friend working under the car behind the closed doors of the garage. It must have been hot and sticky, but the investigators reckoned that the Lebanese preferred the Miami heat to being divebombed by the mosquitoes that were all too common at that time of year. At about 8.30 p.m. Wakil left in his car to pick up a pizza for the two of them. Aboul-Hosn was never again seen in Miami.

Police and fire brigade investigators at the scene accepted that all the evidence pointed to the death being non-criminal. They fiddled with the jack from which the car appeared to have fallen, and the crime laboratory took some photos. The preliminary report by the Dade County Medical Examiner's office stated:

"The deceased jacked up the vehicle and began to work under its rear with an extension light . . . It appeared from the deceased's broken arm that the jack holding the rear of the vehicle slipped, pinning the deceased while the stand under the vehicle punctured the fuel tank. The deceased was burned beyond recognition."

Police enquiries established that Aboul-Hosn had arrived in the USA as an exchange student in 1976. He had apparently come from a mountain village outside Beirut. He took a general course in civil engineering at Jefferson Community College in Louisville, Kentucky, and married

A collapsed jack seemed to have caused the fire, starting a chain of incidents that culminated in the ignition of the fuel pouring from the Chevrolet.

an American girl there – but the marriage lasted only until he obtained his green alien resident's card, and the couple were divorced in 1978.

Luxury home

In 1979 Aboul-Hosn moved to Miami, where he worked first as a waiter and cab driver while attending Miami-Dade Community College. Subsequently he became a salesman for Scharf Land Development Co. A month before the fatal fire, he had rented the luxury home at 9901 SW 138 Street, with its lavishly landscaped garden and oval swimming pool.

The problem facing the police was that of formal identification of the body. Wakil notified Aboul-Hosn's sister Ghada, who was a nursing student in nearby Tampa. Next day the detective in charge of the case, Ray Nazario, asked her if she knew of any dental or medical records that might be of assistance in identifying her brother's body; she said that she did not. Nor did she have any photographs of him smiling.

As there seemed no doubt that the death was an accident, the police accepted the circumstantial evidence of identification of the body as Aboul-Hosn's, and it was released to the Vista Funeral Home in Hialeah, to be prepared for shipping back to Lebanon. But the Medical Examiner's

office, dissatisfied at the lack of formal identification, retained the blackened upper and lower jaws, in the hope that further evidence might later arise to clinch the case. Ghada was given her brother's few possessions and she flew to Lebanon to await the arrival of the body.

Unfortunately, Israel chose that moment to begin 'Operation Peace for Galilee' and war broke out immediately after she arrived. The body remained in the Florida funeral home. After a month, with the situation in Lebanon unimproved, Bassam Wakil reluctantly gave permission for the body to be cremated and he was given the ashes in a wooden box. When Ghada eventually returned, the ashes found their last resting place in the waters of Biscayne Bay. Curiously, none of Aboul-Hosn's friends and family commented on the fact that in the Druze faith, the Muslim sect to which the victim had belonged, cremation is forbidden.

Private investigations

Six months later, John J. Healy arrived in Miami. Healy, a private investigator from New York, had news that caused Ray Nazario to reopen the case. Aboul-Hosn had taken out life and accidental death policies with six different companies over the previous two years. The sum in- ▶

Autopsy Report

Scalp and skull: "The scalp hair has been totally burned off, as well as a large portion of the scalp. Portions of the skull are blackened and partially charred."

Blood: "Internal examination shows no abnormalities, no traces of drugs or alcohol. There is no soot in the airways, but there is a high concentration of carbon monoxide in the blood."

Pugilist pose: "The body is in the characteristic 'pugilist' pose. Thermal fractures of the distal bones of the forearm are noted."

n cases of sudden death, the body or bodies have to undergo post-mortem examination.

With the body from the garage it was a relatively straightforward autopsy, since what had happened seemed apparent from the start. The case was complicated only by the extensive damage to the remains.

The Medical Examiner's report indicated that:

"The body is that of a 5 ft 11 in, 160-lb, well-developed Caucasian male, whose age cannot be compared to the stated age of 34 years due to thermal injury." (Other extracts are shown here.)

The primary cause of death was held to be smoke inhalation.

Although the identity of the deceased was thought to have been established, there was no absolute proof. It was for that reason, fortunately, that the teeth and jaws of the victim were retained.

Teeth: "The teeth are in a good state of repair. No restoration is evident on superficial examination."

Back: "The back is blackened, but two areas of skin are evident, revealing the individual to be a Caucasian."

Body: "The body is extensively charred and exposed muscle is evident over the chest, extremities, abdomen and head. The external genitalia are charred, but are those of a male."

Right: Such was the heat of the fire that the only scraps of the victim's clothes to survive were small shreds trapped beneath the body.

volved totalled $1,270,000. His sister, the named beneficiary, had already received $550,000 from Mutual of Omaha, most of which had already been transferred to Lebanon. In view of the large sums of money involved, and the lack of formal identification of the body, Healy had been retained by the insurance companies to confirm that the dead man was in fact Ezzat Aboul-Hosn. If he was not, then the police would have to start looking for the perpetrator of a massive fraud. More to the point, if the body had not been that of Aboul-Hosn, they were dealing with a murder case.

Healy proceeded to make his own enquiries in Florida. He discovered that Aboul-Hosn had bought the old Vega, saying that he wanted to work on it, only five

Mystery

Murder in the garage: The unanswered

How did the killer organise his crime?

Aboul-Hosn had supposedly been working on his car with a friend for several hours. His friend Wakil had gone to buy some pizzas when the 'accident' occurred. Where was the victim all the time that the two men were working on the car? How did Aboul-Hosn arrange the 'accident', all in the 20 or 30 minutes that the pizza run would have taken? How did he manage to get his victim under the car, conscious or unconscious, in the correct position?

How did he get away?

The first arrivals, neighbours, were on the scene within seconds of the explosion, and the fire department was there in minutes. Ezzat Aboul-Hosn had to get away from the house in a hurry, before the arrival of the first onlookers from across the road. How did he avoid being seen? How did he get out of the country? Had he arranged flights beforehand? Did he use a false name and papers?

How did the jack collapse?

To all outward appearances the bumper jack had slipped, allowing the car to fall. Once it became clear that a murder had been committed, the investigators were faced with some problems. How had the killer arranged for the jack to collapse? Did he use a rope to pull it? How did he arrange for the axle support to pierce the fuel tank?

How was the fire started?

The killer had to ensure that the fire started as he wanted. Did he trust to luck that the hot work lamp would ignite the fuel, or did he start the fire in some other fashion? Did he have to be in the garage to ignite the petrol? If he did start the fire, how did he avoid getting caught up in the conflagration?

days before the fatal fire, although he already owned a new white Gran Prix and had the use of a company Cadillac. Healy interviewed Ghada, who was about to return once more to Lebanon: she confirmed that her brother liked to work on old cars.

Dental search

Since the only surviving evidence in the case, apart from the pathologist's samples, was the jaws taken from the body, Healy set about searching for a dentist who might have treated Aboul-Hosn. He thought that he had succeeded when his enquiries

Left: After the bumper jack collapsed, the car fell and an axle-stand pierced the fuel tank. According to one of the investigating officers, there was no explosion, but once ignited the flow of gasoline served to stoke the fire.

brought to light a set of dental X-rays labelled 'Abdul-Hussan', but he eventually discovered that these belonged to a student at the University of Miami with a similar name.

In Key West, Healy ran to earth Aboul-Hosn's girlfriend. She was still very distressed by the death, which had occurred soon after he had telephoned to arrange to visit her in Key West at the weekend. She said that Ezzat was healthy and never ill, and had "a nice smile"; she did not know of any dentist or physician who might have treated him. Reluctantly, she allowed Healy to take away a single colour Polaroid photograph that showed Aboul-Hosn seated with his sister during a graduation ceremony.

Due to the fact that the winter season was starting in Florida, and that hotel space

and reservations were becoming unavailable, Healy returned to New York. But he had not given up. A little later he flew to Louisville, where Aboul-Hosn had attended college, and there he discovered a full set of Aboul-Hosn's dental X-rays in the possession of Dr Wood Currens at the University of Louisville Dentistry School.

Meanwhile, the Dade County police had been pursuing their own enquiries. On 11 January 1983 the Chief Medical Examiner, Dr Joseph Davis, alerted dental examiner Dr Richard Souviron, who had examined the jaws of the body, and a week later Ray Nazario was told to make sure that the Louisville X-rays were obtained from Dr Currens "before Mr Healy got a hold of them." Aboul-Hosn's driving licence, which he had renewed only a week before the fire, was also found on file. On 21 January the X-rays arrived, and on 24 January Dr Souviron declared that the dead man was certainly not Ezzat Aboul-Hosn.

A case of murder

There was no doubt about it: this was no longer a case of accidental death, but one of murder. But who was the dead man, and what had happened to Ezzat Aboul-Hosn? Scenting an exciting story, reporters from the *Miami Herald* began their own investigation. And on 3 March 1983 Dan Goodgame filed a long report from Btekhnay in Lebanon:

"Ten months after he supposedly burned to death in Miami, backyard mechanic Ezzat M. Aboul-Hosn is home again – a rich man in a small Lebanese mountain village," it began. "He owns two new cars and a truck. His $250,000 villa ▶

questions

How did the victim die?
There was no soot in the victim's lungs, but from the concentration of carbon monoxide in his blood, the Medical Examiner concluded that the victim had died from smoke inhalation. This can happen when a victim dies early in a fire. There was no indication of any other injury, except for the broken arm trapped under the axle. Given that this was murder and not an accident, was the victim unconscious or even dead from carbon monoxide poisoning before the fire was started? If so, how had the murderer done it?

I**t was an almost perfect murder. Police and firemen called to the blazing garage saw just what they were expected to see. As far as anybody knew, Ezzat Aboul-Hosn had suffered a horrific accident while tinkering with his old Chevrolet Vega. Some time later, however, people began to question that explanation. For a man of relatively modest means, the victim's life had been vastly over-insured. The insurance companies wanted definite confirmation of the victim's identity before paying out large sums of money. It was only the persistence of an insurance investigator, searching for that confirmation, which turned the case around. Further examination showed that the charred body, burned beyond all recognition, had not been Ezzat Aboul-Hosn. Knowing that it was murder was one thing. Finding out how it had been done was something else, and investigators were faced with a number of puzzling questions.**

The body was found pinned to the concrete floor by the right rear wing of the collapsed car. One arm had been trapped under the axle. The remains were burned to an unrecognisable crisp. Both police and fire officials on the scene believed the death to be accidental.

Who was the victim?
He was of the same height, race and build as Aboul-Hosn. Nobody had reported seeing such a person in the vicinity prior to the murder and nobody had been reported missing. The teeth could have been a help in identification, except that there were no dental records for comparison. The identity of the body under the car remains a mystery.

Guilty

The last laugh

Below: Teeth were all that could identify the victim. Fortunately, they were retained by the Medical Examiner's office when the rest of the body was released for cremation, and they were available for comparison when the victim's identity was questioned.

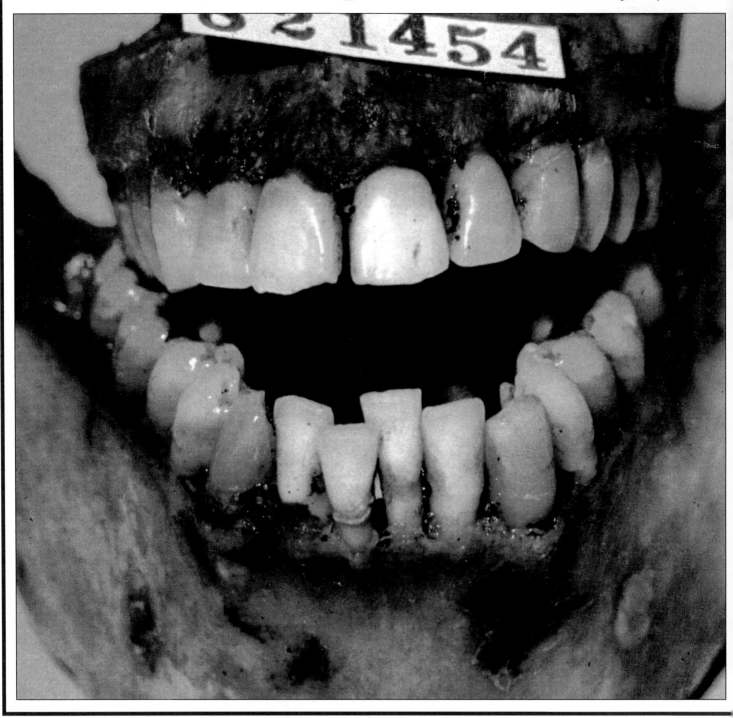

▶ is under construction. He maintains a fat savings account at a local bank. He pays his bills from a book of fancy oversized checks." Goodgame supported his assertion with a photograph of the villa under construction, next door to Aboul-Hosn's family home in the village of Btekhnay.

Ghada confirmed that her brother had faked his death. "I was so hurt and angry that I had been used. I didn't want any of the money. I gave it to him. It's dirty money." She said that Ezzat had fled only

hours before Goodgame arrived. He had taken a taxi to Damascus in Syria, and intended to fly "to Europe, for two years, maybe longer." But villagers suggested that he was in hiding nearby.

Family shame

Unravelling the family connections in the village is impossible – every single one of the 2,500 inhabitants is named Aboul-Hosn – but many expressed concern for 'the

family name'. Said Adnan Aboul-Hosn, an airline pilot: "Some of us think we should turn him over to the US Embassy so he can be tried. And if he did kill someone for this money, he should get the electric chair." But there is no extradition treaty between the USA and Lebanon and Ezzat Aboul-Hosn has apparently remained in contented possession of his ill-gotten gains.

And, 10 years later, the identity of the murdered man has not been established.

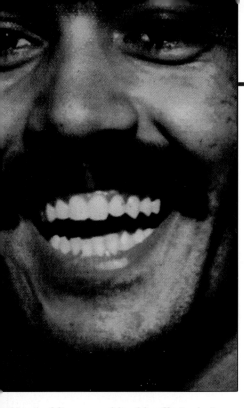

It was the photo on Aboul-Hosn's driving licence which first indicated that he was not the man in the garage.

Above: After a considerable effort, photos of 'Eddie' Aboul-Hosn were found which showed his teeth. When compared with the teeth of the victim of the garage fire, they did not match. The victim was not Aboul-Hosn. What had been accidental death was now murder.

I t is a simple proof of identity. You superimpose the photograph of a skull with a photograph of the live person. If they match, you have made your identification. If they don't match, then the skull is not the remains of the person you suspect it to be.

Photos on record

Ezzat Aboul-Hosn tried to get rid of all of his photographs, but he could do nothing about those on file at various records offices. It was his grinning face on an identity card and on a Florida driving licence which gave him away. As evidence that Aboul-Hosn had committed a near perfect murder, one question remained. Where was he?

Return to Lebanon

Rumours eventually reached Miami that the fugitive was alive. He was living off the ill-gotten gains of his murderous scam back home in Lebanon. With no extradition treaty between the USA and that war-torn country, Ezzat Aboul-Hosn was safe from arrest. He was not safe, however, since many members of his extensive clan thought that he had brought shame on the family.

Police made considerable efforts to match the jaws taken from the body with known dental records of missing persons, but without success. Dr Souviron has pointed out "the detail and thought that criminals will extend in committing such a crime." The victim placed under the car was the same age, race and sex as Aboul-Hosn; great ingenuity was shown in setting up the jack so that death was plausibly an accident; and there is the possibility (suggested by the absence of soot in the victim's airways) that he had been asphyxiated with carbon monoxide before the fire was started. "It's such a fantastically interesting situation," said Dr Davis, the Medical Examiner. "If they ever do find out what happened, I want to know how it was done." □

Sudden inferno leaves mystery

Aboul-Hosn had been covered...

Ghada Aboul-Hosn, a nursing student in Tampa, was the beneficiary of Ezzat's life insurance. The massive size of the policies he had taken out in the previous year aroused insurance company suspicions. At their prompting, the police reopened the case.

'Dead' man ran, but can he hide from angry kin?

Planned home of Ezzat Aboul-Hosn, right, takes shape next to family home in Btekhnay, Lebanon.

Reporters tracked Ezzat Aboul-Hosn down to a Druze village in the Lebanon. When last seen, he was fleeing from relatives who felt he had brought shame on the family.

PETER AND GWENDA DIXON

The deeply wooded cliffs on the south-west tip of Wales are beautiful. In 1989, however, they were the scene of a vicious double killing which remains unsolved.

WHO KILLED THE CLIFFTOP COUPLE?

They were an ordinary couple, camping on the rocky Welsh coast. But a murderous attack cut Peter and Gwenda Dixon's holiday brutally short.

Peter and Gwenda Dixon had been on holiday to the same area of Pembrokeshire every year for 15 years. Their idea of heaven was to spend their days rambling along the wild Welsh coast watching the sea birds and the surf crashing on the rocks below them.

They lived quietly in a suburban semi near Witney in Oxfordshire. Peter, who was 51, was a sales and marketing manager for an electronics firm. Gwenda, 52, worked as a secretary. They had two grown-up children, Peter, who was 27, and his sister Julie, an 18-year-old student.

The Dixons had arrived in Wales on 19 June 1989. They booked into the Howelston Farm campsite at Little Haven and pitched their dark green tent.

On Thursday 29 June at 9.30 a.m. the

Dixons set off from the camp, telling other holidaymakers that they planned to walk along the cliffs towards the village of Dale, overlooking Milford Haven Bay.

Their last walk

They were both dressed in shorts, hiking boots and light summery shirts. They were carrying a camera, a small rucksack and binoculars, with which they hoped to spot a pair of rare peregrine falcons that had nested on the cliffs along that stretch of coast.

The last person to see them alive, another camper, watched them go out of a gate in the corner of the campsite and vanish from view over a mound called Strawberry Hill that leads to the cliff trail.

Because of the free and easy nature of the camp no-one noticed when they failed to return that night. In fact, the alarm was not raised until the following Monday.

The couple had been expected home on Sunday 2 July. They had an arrangement to pick their daughter up at Heathrow airport after a holiday in Cyprus. When they failed to get home in time, their son Tim assumed they had been delayed and collected his sister himself.

But by the next day Tim's concern had grown to alarm and he contacted the police. At the campsite detectives found his parents' dark green canopy tent, its entrance zipped tight, their camp-beds, spare clothes and cooking equipment stored neatly inside exactly as it had been left. The Dixons' car was parked alongside the tent, locked and undisturbed.

The police initially feared that there had been some sort of accident. The Dixons would not have been the first holiday makers to fall to their deaths from the

64

clifftops to the jagged rocks more than 200 feet below.

An intensive search was organised. Police and local volunteers combed the heather and beat bushes along more than 10 miles of thickly wooded coastal paths and rabbit runs. A police spotter helicopter cruised along the cliff face but saw nothing untoward.

It was not until Wednesday 5 July that police tracker dogs led their handlers to a gruesome sight. Hidden in undergrowth, some 20 feet down the side of the steeply sloping cliff, lay two bodies face down. Both had been shot three times in the head and chest at the place where they lay, a fact revealed by the heavy bloodstains.

Whoever had killed Peter and Gwenda Dixon had gone to extreme lengths. The bodies were in such a dangerous spot that the dog handlers who found them feared they might fall to their deaths just getting down to them.

Recovering the bodies

It later took police six hours using safety lines and pulleys to winch stretchers with the bodies strapped to them back up the cliff to the path.

Because of the number of shots fired, the killer, if he had used a conventional double-barrelled gun, would have had to reload his weapon. But he had been careful to collect any spent cartridges and take them away.

Peter Dixon's hands had been bound behind his back using a length of sail cord, probably washed ashore along the coast.

This fact gave rise to the theory that

Missing persons

Above: The Dixons' tent and car were found just as the couple had left them on the Howelston Farm campsite.

Left: Peter and Gwenda Dixon were keen walkers and particularly liked this stretch of the Welsh coast for their holidays. They had planned to buy a home in the area, so they could spend more time here after Peter retired.

O ver the 10 days of their holiday, the Dixons had kept themselves to themselves. Pleasantly tired after their long walks, they would usually be asleep soon after sunset. Other campers became used to seeing their tent dark and apparently deserted, so nobody noticed that they had not returned from their ramble on 29 June. The alarm was only raised by their son when they did not return from their holiday on 2 July as planned.

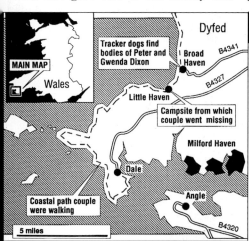

MAIN MAP
Wales

Dyfed

Tracker dogs find bodies of Peter and Gwenda Dixon

Broad Haven B4341

B4327

Little Haven

Campsite from which couple went missing

Milford Haven

Dale

Angle

Coastal path couple were walking

B4320

5 miles

Above: St Anne's Head is a relatively small area, not far from the busy oil port of Milford Haven. Even so, it is generally deserted during the week.

Right: Dog teams checked the fields along the top of the cliffs after the Dixons were reported missing.

Gruesome discovery

T im Dixon reported his parents missing on Monday 3 July. The last time they had been seen, on the morning of the 29th, they had intended walking around St Anne's Head. That part of the Welsh coast is rugged, with rocky cliffs overlooking deep inlets of the sea. Police knew from experience how easy it was for walkers to come to grief in such terrain, so they first concentrated the search along the foot of the cliffs.

It was not until search teams moved along the top of the cliff with dogs that their mutilated bodies were found. It was not an accident: the Dixons had been blasted with a shotgun.

Right: The Dixons were described as "the loveliest couple", without any enemies. It was at first believed they had been killed by a maniac.

DAILY **Mirror**

Friday, July 7, 1989   National Sale: 3,934,721 Incorporating the Daily Record   22p

FIND THE CLIFFTOP MANIAC

Sex beast gunman is hunted

MURDERED: Keep-fit fan Peter Dixon

HOLIDAYMAKERS were warned last night not to walk coastal paths alone after a sex maniac gunned down two cliff-top walkers.

The mutilated bodies of Peter Dixon, 51, and his wife Gwenda, 52, were found on two at St Bride's Bay, in West Wales, on Wednesday. They had been shot.

By IAN CAMERON

more than one killer was involved. Could one man have tied Peter's hands while still covering him with a gun? It seemed unlikely. Injuries on his hands and wrists seemed to indicate a struggle.

Peter's wallet was missing. Again, detectives wondered if this was a deliberate ploy by the killer. The lonely path, tramped only by the occasional hiker, seemed a bizarre place to stage an armed hold-up. And if robbery was the motive, why were valuables including the couple's watches, their camera and the binoculars found scattered further down the cliff side?

An entomologist called in to examine insect eggs that had been laid in the corpses was able to give an accurate time of death. The police were able to find three witnesses who said they heard the sound of gunshots coming from the direction of the cliffs between about 11 and 11.15 a.m. on the day the couple vanished.

Hunt for the killer

The investigators could be sure of only one thing: the Dixons had died on the day they walked off from the camp. The killer had a six-day start.

When Peter Dixon had left the camp he took with him his wallet containing six credit cards, a bank card, his driving licence and a BT charge card. Detectives quickly found out that the bank cash card had been used to make four withdrawals in the days immediately following the murders.

Now police believed they had a lead. A witness came forward to describe a man he had seen using the NatWest cash point in Haverfordwest early on the morning of 1 July.

The witness had been driving through the town centre. He had seen a man wear-

Sketch of man issued in hunt for couple's clifftop killer

By Michael Fleet
Welsh Correspondent

AN ARTIST'S impression of a man wanted for questioning about the murders of cliff walkers Mr Peter Dixon, 51 and his wife, Gwenda, 52, was issued by police yesterday as their son appealed to the killer to give himself up.

Mr Timothy Dixon, 26, was flanked by police leading the investigation as he told the killer: "You cannot be happy with yourself. Why don't you give yourself up to the police? How can you live with yourself with what you have done to my parents?"

The man being sought was described as between 30 and 45, unshaven and untanned. Police fear that he might be armed and dangerous.

"He should not be approached by any member of the public," said Det Chief Supt Clive Jones.

He said the suspect, dressed in shorts and walking boots, had possibly been living rough and had been seen in the region during the three weeks before Mr and Mrs Dixon, of Witney, Oxfordshire, were murdered on the Pembrokeshire cliff path in west Wales.

Mr Jones appealed to two men seen on the cliff at the time the Dixons disappeared 10 days ago to contact police.

Disused houses, barns and outbuildings in the area had been searched. No clues or the shotgun used by the killer had been found. Police had also failed to determine the motive for the killing and had not ascertained the time of death, he added.

Mr Dixon spoke yesterday of the affection that his parents had for the remote part of the world where they were killed.

"It is very sad this should have happened to them in an area they loved."

He said local people had been a tremendous support, and that he planned to return to the area for holidays in memory of his parents.

"My whole family is absolutely devastated. It is very difficult thinking ahead and it has been hell imagining how we are going to pick up the threads of our lives."

Mr Timothy Dixon and Det Chief Supt Clive Jones at the press conference

A sketch of the suspect

Mrs Gwenda Dixon

Mr Peter Dixon

Daily Telegraph
11 July 1989

Above: Still following the lone killer theory, police issued a description and artist's impression of a scruffy man who had been seen hanging around the area in the weeks before the killing.

ing shorts, a T-shirt and hiking boots using the cash dispenser at the bank. He was wheeling an old-fashioned black gentleman's bicycle with straight handlebars. He was scruffy, with long hair, sun-tanned and unshaven. He was thought to be between 30 and 45 years old, between five feet eight and six feet in height, and carrying a small rucksack over his shoulder.

The police had also found witnesses who had seen a similar-looking man with a bike

Murder scene

The bodies of Peter and Gwenda Dixon were not found during the first two days of the search because they had been well hidden. The brush-covered cliffs of St Anne's Head slope very steeply, and after the Dixons had been slaughtered, their murderer — or murderers — had taken the bodies part-way down the slope and hidden them behind some thick undergrowth. This was a very perilous task — the police recovery teams took several hours to reach the bodies and bring them back to the path safely.

Right: It might seem odd that two people could be blasted with a shotgun in broad daylight without anybody seeing or hearing anything. However, the remoteness of the clifftop where the couple died meant that the killer or killers could do their evil work without being discovered. Then they could hide the bodies behind bushes (right inset) well down the side of the cliff.

hanging around the centre of Pembroke the day the Dixons died. And a man fitting the same description had been spotted in Marloes village near St Bride's Bay six miles from the murder scene on Wednesday 28 June, the day before the murders. There was a second sighting of him later the same morning at St Bride's crossroads. In both sightings he had been with a younger, fair-haired man.

Working on the theory that he may have been living rough, detectives checked every barn, shed, railway arch and disused building across the county looking for signs, but found nothing. They even appealed for tourists who had been in the area at the time to check their holiday snaps in case he was in the background.

Suspect disappears

It was to no avail. The cyclist who had been so conspicuous in the days leading up to and immediately after the murders and his fair-haired friend had vanished. There were no more withdrawals using Peter Dixon's cash card. The scruffy 'wild man' suspect had completely disappeared.

Detective Chief Superintendent Jones said: "I am sure that there is someone out there who saw something that was highly significant without realising it at the time. It is impossible to believe that the killer was in the area that day and was seen by no-one else."

The most intriguing lead of all came to detectives late in October 1989. Two workmen who had gone out on to the cliff path to dig a hole for a new footpath sign found a collection of electrical wiring and switches buried in the ground.

Anti-terrorist officers needed only a quick glance to recognise the type of components used by the IRA to make booby-trap bombs. There were enough there to make 10 such devices.

Within 24 hours they had spoken to a local ornithologist who regularly tramped the cliff path. The man was highly observant and knew the area like the back of his hand. He had noticed a recently dug patch of ground and lead detectives straight to it.

Terrorist weapons unearthed

With explosives officers standing by, the detectives dug into the reddish brown soil and found a massive dump of terrorist weapons. The cache included five pistols, three AK-47 assault rifles, hundreds of rounds of ammunition, five hand grenades and nearly 100 lb of Semtex. There was also a shotgun.

Police had long suspected that the IRA were smuggling arms and explosives across the Irish sea to Wales at night using fishing boats. Could the tiny jetty at the base of the cliff be the landing point?

If that was the case, as seemed highly

Too many suspects, not enough evidence

As well as the hunt for the scruffy man believed to have been spotted using Peter Dixon's cash cards, detectives quickly found themselves trying to check out a number of strange incidents and theories.

One possibility was that the Dixons had stumbled upon drug smugglers, and were killed because they had seen too much. At the foot of the cliffs where they died was a small and rarely used jetty, the only one on that part of the coast. A steep and overgrown path ran down to it.

Drug smuggling

The West Wales coast has been used many times by drug runners but the clifftop path was 200 feet above a rocky and treacherous piece of coast.

Inspector Dai Davies said: "We have considered the possibility of drug smugglers, but that particular piece of coast is hardly a suitable venue for landing drugs at any time, even in broad daylight."

The strange case of some mysterious divers has also left police baffled. Workmen who had been on the cliff path on the day of the murders came forward to tell detectives about a group of frogmen they had seen in St Bride's Bay diving from a small yellow fibreglass boat with an outboard engine.

Mysterious boat

Police checked with local diving enthusiasts and found that pleasure scuba divers rarely used the bay as the conditions were unsuitable. Despite countrywide appeals the divers in the yellow boat have

never been traced.

Another lead came from another couple who had walked the cliff trail in the days before the murder. They told detectives of a wild-eyed 'weirdo' who had suddenly leapt out at them from the undergrowth on the cliff path. He had shouted at them about the Welsh being driven from their native land by the English before running away down the path.

He was described as being about 40, and looking slim and fit. Was he the same 'wild man' spotted in the area and at the cash point with the old black bicycle?

Radio enthusiast

Another lead came from Mr Dixon's hobby of ham radio. The former RAF electronics specialist had installed a powerful set in his car. Police were able to trace at least nine amateur radio enthusiasts who had conversed with him over the air in the days before he died.

One told police he thought he had cut in on a transmission in which Mr Dixon made arrangements to meet one of the radio enthusiasts called 'Tom'.

Who did he meet?

A farmer told police that Mr. Dixon had asked permission to cross his land to reach the remains of an old World War II airfield, where he said he was going to meet someone.

Could these events hold clues to the case? In the end all lines of inquiry petered out for lack of further information.

Police followed numerous leads, and considered a number of other crimes that might have been linked to the case, but like the search for the scruffy man at the start, all lines of questioning came to nothing.

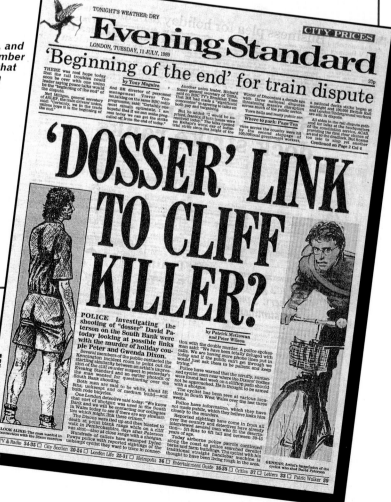

likely, was it possible that the Dixons had died because on that June day they had stumbled on an IRA arms smuggling operation or surprised terrorists burying or digging up their equipment?

The head of the Anti-Terrorist Squad, Commander George Churchill-Coleman, was sure members of a Provisional IRA active service unit would return to collect their stores and decided to mount a special operation to capture them. News of the finds was still a tightly kept secret.

The police took away the guns and explosives and filled in the hole. For eight weeks a team of crack surveillance officers hid in the undergrowth overlooking the spot in freezing rain and gale-force winds day and night.

A week before Christmas they were rewarded. Officers using night sights spotted two men padding along the cliff path. They carried spades – and a shotgun.

IRA men arrested

When the IRA men started to dig the police sprang the ambush. One warning shot was fired into the air by police before the IRA men were overpowered. Welsh police liaised with Scotland Yard and the RUC in Belfast and discovered the arrested men were both top Provisional IRA men.

Some of their movements had been charted. They were known to have been in Britain in the months before the killings and

Tim Dixon and his sister Julie address a press conference, appealing to the killer to give himself up, but to no avail. The murder of the Dixons remains a mystery.

had rented a holiday chalet in the area in September, two months after the murders.

But police intelligence specialists could not pinpoint where they had been in June at the actual time the Dixons were killed. Neither of the men fitted the description of the 'wild man' or any other people seen in the area at the right time. But the two men were almost certainly not the only IRA men who had been in the area.

In keeping with the IRA code, both men arrested on the clifftop refused to answer police questions. At the Old Bailey in 1990 the two IRA men were jailed for 30 years for conspiring to cause explosions.

Welsh detectives later visited them in their prison cells at Full Sutton maximum security jail in Yorkshire to question them about the Dixon murders, but the men still defiantly refused to answer any questions.

Inspector Dai Davies of Dyfed-Powys police said: "Whether it was the IRA, drug smugglers, a robber or just an armed head case we do not know. The Dixon murders remain a great mystery." □

An IRA connection?

Police search the area near the murder scene where a terrorist arms cache was discovered. Were the Dixons killed by the IRA?

The killing of the Dixons appeared senseless, but investigators felt it was more than a maniac gunman making a random killing. Could the couple have stumbled across something they should not have seen? Three months later this became a real possibility with the discovery of a terrorist arms cache not far from the murder site. This was typical of the kind of spot the IRA would use to smuggle in weapons, and they certainly have all of the ruthless disregard for human life shown by the killers of the Dixons. Maybe Peter and Gwenda were two more innocent victims of the troubles in Northern Ireland.

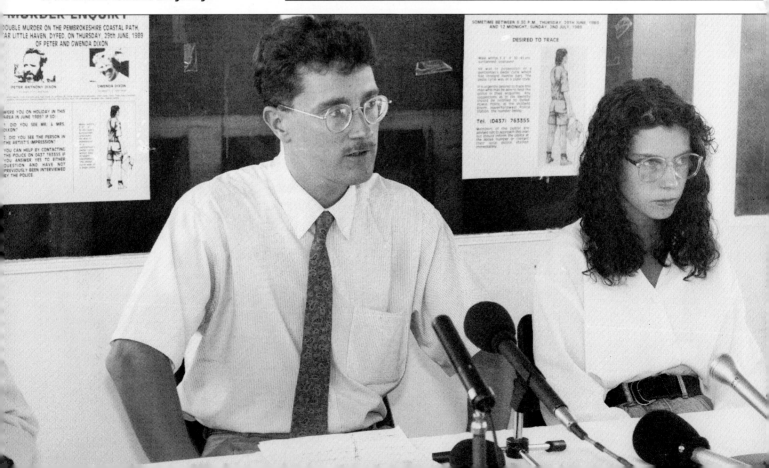

SECRET GRAVE EXPOSES
EVIL KILLER

William Jennings' three-year old son Stephen disappeared without trace in 1962. But it was not until 1988 that Jennings' secret was exposed.

When the father of three-year-old Stephen Jennings reported him missing in the bitterly cold December of 1962, the entire community in and around the village of Lower Gomersal in West Yorkshire became involved in what was to be the largest police operation of the year.

The search for the child proved fruitless, but the memory of the little boy's disappearance lingered on. When, more than 25 years later, a man walking his dog discovered a tiny skeleton concealed beneath stones beside a remote path, the name of Stephen Jennings leapt immediately into the minds of local people and police.

At 4 p.m. on 12 December 1962, William Jennings reported at Gomersal police station that his three-year-old son, Stephen, had been missing since 11 that morning. Jennings had been looking after Stephen, his four-year-old brother Paul, and two-year-old sister Susan, while Eileen Jennings, their mother, had taken the baby of the family, four-month-old Barry, to the local clinic.

Stephen is missing

When Eileen returned to the family's cramped terraced council house at 5 Cross Street, Stephen was not at home. Her husband told her that the children had all gone out to play at a neighbour's, but only Paul and Susan had returned. Three meals had been prepared for the children, three lollipops bought at the local shop, but Stephen was missing.

The search mounted by the West Riding police force from Gomersal and Cleckheaton police stations was a major operation, although before many hours were up there was little hope of finding the child alive. A local church became the centre of operations, and a refreshment station was set up

Above: Stephen Jennings smiles for the camera in 1962.

Below: Local villagers joined police in a massive search of the area. Foremost among the searchers was Stephen's father, William.

Below: William and Eileen Jennings pictured at the time of Stephen's disappearance. They had an unsavoury reputation in the village because of the way they treated their children.

in a pub. Over 60 police, including dog handlers, were involved. Scores of volunteers joined the police teams, including many men who would join in after finishing the night shift at the local textile mills.

The searchers were faced with an old industrial landscape pocked with ancient mineshafts, criss-crossed with abandoned railway lines, and containing a number of water sites such as reservoirs, culverts and dammed mill ponds where a body could lie undetected. The searchers worked their way through railway sidings, old barns, disused wells and industrial premises both old and in use. Eventually the team would dig over allotments and drain dams. From the beginning they were severely hampered by the savagely cold weather of a winter that was the worst in living memory.

Between December 1962 and March 1963 the ground in the region was frozen solid. Two young police constables taking part in the operation, Tony Ridley, with three years' service, and Brian Prendergast, who joined the search on his first day of active duty, recall braziers kept alight in the streets, and searchers bundled in extra clothing, the police wearing pyjamas and tracksuits under their uniforms, Both men would take important roles as senior police officers a quarter of a century later when the case was reopened.

Searching in the snow

Just after Christmas it snowed, covering the area in a layer that would not thaw for the next two months. The search had become impossible, and it was called off temporarily.

From the first day there were members of the police and the public who were convinced that 25-year-old William Jennings

Child abuse

Some of the investigating police officers were certain that Jennings targeted Stephen for ill-treatment because he was convinced he was not the boy's father. He also meted out savage treatment to Barry, who had certainly been conceived while Jennings was in prison. Paul and Susan, despite their general scruffiness and poor nutrition, were treated as favourites, and never physically assaulted.

Injured children

In July 1962 Stephen was admitted to Dursley General Hospital with badly scalded feet. Father and son had been alone in the house when it happened. No charges were made. In January 1963, after Stephen's disappearance, Barry was admitted to Batley General Hospital with cut lips. The following month he was treated for a fractured femur.

had killed Stephen and disposed of the body. Two women independently reported seeing Jennings carrying a sack containing something bulky on the day of the toddler's disappearance. Both William and Eileen Jennings were questioned on and off over a

It was a cheerless Christmas in the Jennings' house two weeks after Stephen went missing. But it was rarely a happy home to start with.

Two more sons, Derek and Mark, were born in 1964 and 1965. In April 1965 a babysitter reported to the police that Barry was in a critical physical condition. He was found emaciated in his cot, while the other children were in good condition. William and Eileen Jennings each received 18 months' imprisonment for neglect.

Digging up the bones

Stephen's fate remained unknown until 1988, when an inquisitive Jack Russell terrier dug up a human skull near the old railway embankment at Eddercliffe. The dog's owner could remember the search over 25 years ago.

period of weeks, and the police took William in for more intense questioning for three and four days at a time. He stuck adamantly to his story, voicing the opinion that gypsies might have abducted the boy, and making much of the fact that Stephen's Christmas presents were being kept at home ready for his return. William also took part in the search on several days, when he was not in custody.

Left: The police search for Stephen Jennings was hampered by the severe weather conditions. The whole area was soon blanketed by a heavy fall of snow.

When the thaw began in March 1963 the search was resumed, and it carried on for a further two weeks, often going back over ground already covered looking for disturbed earth, and seeking out nooks and crannies where a child's body might be concealed. The possibility of there being a disused well at 5 Cross Street was explored, but without success. Gradually the investigation tailed off. Later, whenever potential clues such as disturbed earth came to light, the police and CID would investigate.

Suspicion of murder

The impact the disappearance had made on the local community never completely faded, and the strong suspicion that a murder had been committed lingered on over the years. The press fuelled speculation every time a child disappeared. At the time of the Moors Murders case in 1965, Stephen Jennings's name was added for a while to the list of missing children who were possible victims of Ian Brady and Myra Hindley. Each year, around Christmas, journalists visited Eileen Jennings to provide themselves with 'human interest'

stories for the holiday season.

Twenty-five years and four months after the little boy had disappeared, a telephone call to Heckmondwike police station reopened the Stephen Jennings case. Just after 6 p.m. on Thursday 7 April 1988, Malcolm Burton, a local man who had taken part in the original searches, was walking his Jack Russell terrier along a little-used path running up an old railway embankment at Eddercliffe, about three-quarters of a mile from the old Jennings' home in Lower Gomersal. Recalling the occasion later, Burton said, "We had got on to the footpath when Mac started growling and barking in the undergrowth. . . . I called him, but he refused to come out, so I went to see what he had found. When I bent down to put the lead on him I saw what he had unearthed." At first Malcolm Burton thought the dog had found a doll's head, but on shifting a stone he saw that there was a small human skull and other bones. He immediately remembered the day Stephen went missing.

Brian Prendergast, who had spent his first day on duty as a young police constable searching for Stephen Jennings, was now a Detective Inspector with the Batley police. Contacted immediately after Burton's phone call, he too thought at once of

Constant cruelty

The Jennings family were always outsiders in the close-knit West Yorkshire community they entered in the early 1960s. This was not an affluent area, but there was considerable pride in work and family, and the anarchic hand-to-mouth existence of the Jennings family, compounded by William's thieving and the neglect of the children, went totally against the grain.

Physical abuse

The Jennings children were frequently seen scantily dressed around the village. They were dirty, and often hungry enough to beg for food and even eat scraps put out for the birds. Villagers gave clothes and food to the family. The villagers grew fond of the amazingly resilient children, but were disturbed at the signs of physical abuse. Neighbours reported a succession of cuts and bruises. On 10 September 1962 Stephen was seen walking around the village wearing nothing but a short vest, without footwear in below-freezing conditions; he was bruised, and had congealed blood on his face.

Thieving father

Antipathy towards the father was exacerbated by a succession of petty thefts of items such as coal and potatoes, which he was suspected of bearing off in the sack he frequently carried, and which probably contained Stephen's body on the day he disappeared.

Eileen Jennings and her husband were both jailed in 1965 after a babysitter reported them to the police for their cruelty to Stephen's half-brother Barry.

Grave site clues

Dr John Hunter, senior lecturer in archaeology at Bradford University, first thought about applying archaeological methods to certain police investigations in 1965, when he saw press photos of police digging for victims of the Moors Murderers. He explained that, for archaeologists, the key to a burial lies in its context.

Soil traces

Anything done on or in the ground leaves a series of traces, and changes to natural soil formation. By systematically studying layers of earth as they are exposed in the dig, and analysing the relationship between them, archaeologists can gather often quite detailed information about past events. The trained archaeologist also picks up information from undulations in the land, changes in vegetation and varying levels of growth. The subtle evidence revealed in this way is lost if remains are removed from the site to a laboratory before being properly examined.

Concealed body

In the Stephen Jennings case, archaeological methods revealed that the body had been deliberately hidden on the surface under a layer of stones, and that it had been wrapped in something like a sack.

The infamous garden at 10 Rillington Place, where the evil sex killer Christie buried his victims. There, as in the case of Stephen Jennings, the soil and vegetation around the grave revealed vital forensic clues.

the missing boy. After visiting the site, posting a guard, and urging Malcolm Burton to secrecy, he contacted his old colleague Tony Ridley, now a Detective Superintendent on the Kirklees force.

The tasks facing Ridley, who was put in charge of the reopened investigation, and Prendergast, as his second in command, were to try to identify the remains, establish a cause of death, find as many as possible of the original witnesses, and, most important of all, establish the whereabouts of William Jennings, all without alerting him. If Jennings were indeed the murderer, it would be essential to catch him off his guard when first making contact with him; then, they might be able to obtain a confession before he had time to consider that, if he stuck to his old story, the charges probably would not stick.

Archaeological team

Examination of the guarded site began the next day, Friday 8 April. Instead of removing the remains straight to a police laboratory for forensic analysis, Detective Superintendent Ridley brought in an archaeological team from Bradford University, under the direction of Dr John Hunter, to carry out the excavation. Ten weeks before, Ridley had been involved in a case where human bones had been discovered in a drained mill dam. These bones had probably been the remains from a flooding tragedy that had killed more than 90 workmen 150 years previously. Ridley's boss, Detective Chief Superintendent Kevin Cooper, had remarked that if another case of long-buried bones ever arose they should contact Dr John Hunter, who had been studying the possibilities of forensic archaeology, a science that had never been put into practice in Britain.

The archaeological team painstakingly excavated the bones of the small skeleton, with the scenes of crime photographer taking pictures at every stage. They were able to establish that the body had been laid on top of the turf and covered with stones. Later the dry stone wall against which the body had been placed had collapsed to cover it further. The archaeological analysis also revealed that the body had probably been contained in a wrapping such as a sack. Nearly all the bones of the skeleton had remained together, roughly in position; with most unwrapped bodies decaying in the open, the bones would have been scattered by animals or wind and rain.

Sandals found

Nothing remained of any sack or of any clothing, which had all rotted away. However, the archaeologists did discover a pair of leather sandals with the skeleton. These were in a good state of preservation, and

Right: Police repeatedly questioned William Jennings after Stephen's disappearance. They knew his history of child abuse and strongly suspected him, but Jennings stuck to his story. By the time the body was discovered in 1988, he was divorced from Stephen's mother and was living in Wolverhampton.

Below: Police held back the news that Stephen's grave had been located here in these bushes. Had it been found in 1962, Stephen's killer would probably have gone to the gallows.

Killer's confession

Arrested at his new home in Wolverhampton, William Jennings was driven to the police station. Sitting next to Detective Inspector Prendergast, he kept repeating the same lies he had told since the night of his son's disappearance. But towards the end of the journey, Jennings finally admitted that he had killed Stephen himself.

matched exactly the description of the sandals Stephen had been wearing when William Jennings reported him missing.

Once the bones had been recovered, they were removed for forensic tests by the Home Office pathologist, at the Department of Forensic Pathology at St James's Hospital in Leeds. Dr Somasundram Siva did a reconstruction of the skeleton and, with the aid of an odontologist, was able to confirm that it was that of a child of three or three-and-a-half years of age. A greenstick fracture to one wrist corresponded to an injury Stephen was known to have suffered not long before his disappearance. The age of the skeleton, the fracture of the wrist, the sandals, the geographical location of the bones and the lack of any other unsolved disappearance of young children in the area all amounted to a considerable body of evidence that the remains were those of Stephen Jennings.

Dr Siva's team were also able to tell the story of the boy's final moments in grim detail. At or around the time of death Stephen had suffered a series of violent fractures, eight in all, to his ribs. According

Like father, like son

In April 1990, in a riot at Dartmoor prison, Barry, the son Eileen Jennings had conceived while her husband was in jail, died in his barricaded and burnt-out cell at the age of 27. After William and Eileen had served their 18-month sentences for neglecting him in 1965, Barry remained in care, while the other children returned to their mother.

Knife attack

In November 1989 Barry was given a six-year sentence at Oxford Crown Court for robbery and wounding, which involved a savage knife attack on four people. In a letter he had smuggled out of prison, Barry claimed that on learning of his stepfather's conviction for murdering Stephen, he had a breakdown that culminated in two suicide attempts, followed by the knife attacks that had put him inside.

to Dr Siva, "Those fractures were the result of forces similar to what we find in road traffic accidents, or the force we would get by falling perhaps 30, 40, 50 or 60 feet. I think they were quite consistent with being punched from behind or kicked from behind."

The attempt to trace members of the Jennings family, their neighbours and other possible witnesses was made more difficult by the fact that no file existed on the original investigation, as it had been lost during a reorganisation of the police station. Several people who had been contacted in 1962, including policemen, were now dead. Cross Street had been pulled down in the early 1970s, to be replaced with modern bungalows. The Jennings family had moved out of Lower Gomersal in 1964, and William and Eileen had separated after serving joint sentences for neglect in 1965-66. They were divorced in 1972. The investigating team discovered that William Jennings was living in Albrighton, Wolverhampton, with a new partner he had contacted via a lonely hearts advertisement in the 1970s.

Police activity

On the weekend of 9-10 April 1988 a police team of four drove down to Albrighton; they checked out Jennings' address, to make sure he was in residence, then took some photographs, before returning to Batley.

On Monday 11 April a phone call from the *Spenborough Guardian*, a local paper, brought the fear that the story might break before Jennings could be arrested. The reporter, who had noticed police activity in the search area, was brought in, and agreed to keep quiet, having been promised a scoop when the time was right for the police to go public.

At 6.30 a.m. on Wednesday 13 April Detective Inspector Prendergast left Batley police station in a car together with a Detective Sergeant and a Detective Constable. The plan was to arrest Jennings and question him on the way back north, hoping for a confession. In another car was a task force of four, who would search the house after the arrest.

Confrontation with Jennings

Much would depend on Jennings' initial reaction. The policemen could not question him unless he volunteered information. At 8.30 a.m. they were at the house in Albrighton. The curtains were still drawn. They knocked on the door, which was opened by a woman. The detectives identified themselves and entered the house, going upstairs to the bedroom, where Brian Prendergast recognised William Jennings getting out of bed, despite the passage of years. Prendergast identified himself, and said, "Stephen Jennings has been found."

Jennings' reply was: "Have you found him up on the moors?" This indicated to the team that Jennings had seen the press coverage of the inquest on Pauline Reed, one of the Moors Murders victims, the previous day. He was obviously thinking fast. Brian Prendergast went on to arrest him for the murder of Stephen Jennings in December 1962. This was a calculated risk, since he was not even being arrested 'on suspicion', and could walk free in 24 hours unless he decided to make an admission.

They set off back for Batley, with Brian Prendergast sitting in the back of the car with the handcuffed Jennings, and the two other CID men in the front. After cautioning Jennings, Brian Prendergast told him he knew very well that the remains had not been found on the moors. Jennings repeated the explanations he had given 25 years previously, claiming that he believed gypsies had taken the boy away. Then he began to cry.

Jennings' confession

It was a one-and-a-half-hour journey to Batley. Jennings was silent for 20 minutes, then said he did not mind talking, because he wanted to prove he had not done it. Asked if he had spoken to his ex-wife about Stephen, he replied, "Well, it's nothing to do with her." The team had a glimmer of hope. Then Jennings sat silent. With only 20 minutes of the journey left, he was still

silent. Then he said, "I'm a bastard. How could I do it and say nothing?"

Gradually William Jennings told his version of events to Brian Prendergast. The men were of similar age. The policeman called Jennings 'Bill', and spoke to him politely. The two younger men called him 'Mr Jennings'. As Jennings spoke, one of the men in the front took notes.

"I knocked him through the banister. He fell down the stairs. I went to him, but he didn't die at the time. I picked him up, took him to a bed. He was breathing funny. Then he stopped breathing. I breathed into his mouth. I thumped his chest. He stopped. I watched him die. Only a couple of minutes. I couldn't do anything else for him. I panicked. I didn't know when the

Detective Superintendent Ridley (left) and Detective Inspector Prendergast led the reopened investigation that finally secured the conviction of William Jennings.

How a father hid his son's body

Forensic evidence made a mockery of William Jennings' story. The horrific injuries revealed by the autopsy showed that Jennings had beaten his three-year-old son to death. To conceal his appalling crime, he had bundled the body into a potato sack and carried it to the overgrown path by the railway embankment. He covered the body with stones, hoping to bury the truth as well.

Evil Mind

Thief turned child killer

Born on 9 July 1937, William Leonard Jennings came from the Midlands, and had a history of petty crime going back to his childhood. He went to approved school at the age of 10, again at 15, and then on to Borstal for three years. He worked sporadically as a labourer, but could never keep a job for long, returning always to burglary and theft.

Habitual criminal

Between the ages of 10 and 25 he was more often inside prison than out. At the age of 20, while serving six months for larceny, he was allowed out to marry Mary Eileen Roper, who was five months pregnant with their first child, Paul. Paul was born in April 1958, and Stephen was born in June 1959, while William Jennings was in prison at Southampton for larceny.

In February 1960 Jennings went down for three years, for burglary, at Dudley. In August that year Eileen gave birth to Susan. The family moved, with William still in prison, to a one-up, one-down back-to-back terraced house in Lower Gomersal, near Leeds. The original idea was to get away from William Jennings, but when he was released in April 1962 he joined them at 5 Cross Street.

wife was coming back. I put him in a sack and took him into a field at the back. I put him at the bottom of a wall and put stones on him."

At 7.28 p.m., in the presence of a solicitor, Jennings was charged with the murder of Stephen. He said nothing. At Batley Magistrates Court the following week Jennings thanked the officers for the way they had dealt with him, saying they had behaved like gentlemen. The following month he was bailed on tight conditions.

Liar to the end

At his trial in May 1989 Jennings repeated the version of events he had given in the car, trying for a manslaughter verdict, on the grounds that Stephen had died after being beaten in punishment for soiling the bed and then falling down the stairs. However, expert evidence asserted that the violence of the injuries inflicted on the boy would have killed him outright. William Jennings was found guilty of murder on 23 May 1989 at Leeds Crown Court, and sentenced to life imprisonment. An appeal was dismissed. Had he been charged and found guilty at the time of Stephen's death in 1962 he might well have been hanged. □

Yorkshire Evening Post 24 May 1989

Stephen Jennings was only six months old when his father went back to prison. He was released in April 1962, and murdered the boy eight months later.

Left: William Jennings would have kept his guilty secret until he died, but for the chance discovery of his son's secret grave.

Right: In 1989 William Jennings, now 52, was convicted of murdering his three-year-old son and was sentenced to life imprisonment.

Deadly secret finally caught with killer

By DAVID BRUCE Crime Reporter

WILLIAM LEONARD JENNINGS lived with the deadly secret of his tiny son's death for 25 years.

But justice — and truth — finally caught up with him at Leeds Crown Court when the full horror of Stephen's tragic death became an open book.

Since the bitterly cold winter's day in December 1962 when three-year-old Stephen Jennings was reported missing, William Jennings had consistently denied any knowledge of his son's fate.

He claimed he must have wandered off — or had been abducted by gipsies.

But his lies were finally exposed by a quirk of fate in April last year, more than 25 after Jennings had buried Stephen's body in a field at Eddercliffe, Cleckheaton.

Printer Malcolm Burton was walking across the field when his dog unearthed part of Stephen's skeleton under a clump of undergrowth and trees.

That was to be the start of a police operation which finally solved the m...

and two of his other children out to play to a neighbour's and he had stayed at home, making lunch for the family. His wife had taken their fourth child, Barry, to the doctors.

In spite of intensive searches by police and villagers, no trace of Stephen was found.

However, two years later — by which time the couple had had their sixth child and had moved to a new home in Second Avenue, Hightown, Liversedge — William and Eileen Jennings appeared in court together.

They were charged with neglecting Barry, who was then three...

75

The Chorus Girl
MYSTERY

The discovery of a dismembered skeleton in a disused lead mine near Swansea was to cast light on a murder mystery from nearly 40 years before.

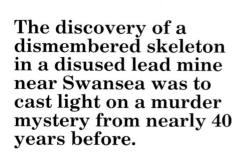

Above left: Murder investigations are like puzzles, and the remains found in an old mine were more puzzling than most. The mute gaze of the skeleton from the cave posed a number of questions. How had the body got there? Who was it? When did he or she die? Was it a suspicious death?

Three young pot-holers were exploring the ventilation shaft of an ancient lead mine on Brandy Cove, a few miles from Swansea. Their route through a small tunnel leading from one of the mine's chambers was blocked by a large stone slab. Levering it aside, they found a human skeleton.

One of the strangest and certainly the longest-running murder investigations took place in a South Wales beauty spot, Caswell Bay, on the Gower coast near Swansea. In 1961, three young pot-holers exploring an old lead mine on the cliffs of Brandy Cove, adjacent to Caswell Bay, found a skeleton hidden behind a large slab of rock

The bones were recovered from the mine by the police and the pot-holers and were taken to the Home Office Forensic Science Laboratory in Cardiff, where they were examined by Dr Lester James, the Home Office Pathologist, and Mr Brian Morgan, forensic scientist.

The bones formed a virtually complete skeleton, which had been sawn into three approximately equal lengths. There were saw cuts through the lower part of each thigh bone and across both upper arms below the shoulders and the spine and shoulder blades. On the upper arm bones there were several partial saw cuts, where the saw had obviously been removed and had been unable to find the same cut because of the entry of muscle. Between these tentative cuts and the main cuts, there were a series of scratches from the teeth of the saw as it skidded from one place to the other. These marks provide a mute reminder of the desperation and per-

Evidence

Her last possessions

Some items of jewellery were found with the skeleton. Wedding and engagement rings bore hallmarks from 1912 and 1918, indicating that the earliest time the body could have been dumped was just after World War I.

haps panic that must have affected the perpetrator in the commission of his crime.

But who had the victim been? How old was he or she? How long had the body been lying in that old lead mine? If the body had been there for a very long time, police could have been looking at an archaeological find. On the other hand, it is quite possible for a body to become completely skeletonised within a few years of death, in which case this was probably murder. When had the crime been committed?

Personal possessions

˙With the body were some mouldering remnants of clothing and sacking, some jewellery, a seven-inch brass chain and a celluloid hair clasp. The clasp still contained some hair, which the forensic scientist said showed no signs of artificial waving or dying and was mid-brown in colour. There were patches of green staining on the bones due to copper contamination from some of the brass jewellery.

A wedding and an engagement ring were present, and research into the hallmarks indicated that the latest dates were 1912 and 1918. There were also some gilt-copper tassels, which the Costume Department at the National Museum of Wales indicated were worn on the end of a stole, fashionable about 1920.

Dr James described the bones as those of a young female, from the configuration of the head and pelvis. The height was estimated at about five feet four inches, both by measuring the skeleton overall after re-assembly and also by calculation from individual limb bones.

The age was estimated by assessing the growth areas in the bones, which appeared to have recently reached their conclusion, suggesting an age in the middle-20s: X-ray examination showed that the skeleton was that of a fully mature adult but that full maturation had only just occurred. There were three wisdom teeth, which suggested that she was over 20, and a complete absence of fusion of the bones of the skull and palate.

X-ray also showed that two bones at the

Boys stumble on a 40-year myste

GOWER SKELETON M BE MAMIE

Clue to the chorus girl who vanished

WHERE IS MAMIE?
BEAUTIFUL SWANSEA GIRL
AN ACTRESS

MISS MAMIE STUART

FLASHBACK to a report in 1920 of Mamie Stuart's d appearance.

FORENSIC science experts in Cardiff were today examining a skeleton which may solve a 40-year-old mystery—the mystery of Mamie Stewart.

Mamie, a 26-year-old chorus girl, vanished in 1920. And the leton—discovered in a disused lead mine in Gower yesterday— be hers.

e Skeleton was found near Brandy Cove by three Bishopston youth, John Graham Jones and Colin McNamarra. Mamie Stuart was a chorus girl South Shields, who went to Swansea on several occasions with a troupe of rs. In 1918 she went through a form of marriage with a man who was dy married. For six months she lived in a house in Trafalgar Terrace, ansea.

She disappeared about the end of 1919, seven months afore the man was sentenced to 18 months hard labour for bigamy.

At his trial the man denied e had ill-used the girl or that had threatened to commit ide.

he police organised a untry-wide search for Mamie uart, who was said to have "gold tooth and a scar." She was known to have left Sunderland on November 5, 1919. Her parents received a letter from her on November 12. It was postmarked Ty Llonwydd, Newton, Mumbles.

Festive greetings

their silence

She also sent them a Christ-as greeting by telegram from ansea on December 24. at was the last they heard om her.

Mamie was believed to have een seen alive for the last time n Newton at the end of December. Wild rumours swept the area for many weeks. Many letters were received by he police and local newspapers erin formation. One letter a spiritualist in aimed he was mie. her in the wrote, "I cate small for polic uths retur

eye tooth missing. The police, however, would not say whether an eye tooth was missing from the skeleton.

Nor would they comment on the suggestion that there was a mark on the side of the skull which could have been caused by a dog bite.

Mamie was known to have had such an injury. Mamie Stewart's description, issued by the police in 1920, said she was 5ft, 4in, tall.

Commenting on a report that the skeleton had been "sawn up," a police spokesman said the bones were in pieces, but whether this was due to their being sawn up or the results of disintegration through age would not be known until the forensic scientists had made their report.

And the youths were exploring an old air shaft of a disused lead mine and squeezed through a fault in the rock strata at the bottom.

A skull among the boulders

This led them into an ante-chamber of the mine and to a low tunnel leading from it.

They found the tun blocked by a large stone After much effort they the slab and saw a hu among some boulders

They informed the because the entre small for police uths retur

BRITISH SHIP BLOWS

The disappearance of Mamie Stuart was big news in 1920. Forty years later, the local papers connected the recently discovered skeleton with the former chorus girl.

base of the skull had recently joined, which indicated that it was unlikely that she was more than 28.

Clearly, the crime had occurred in the years immediately after World War I. The next stage in the investigation was to see if

there were any missing persons cases from that period which involved a young woman in her mid-20s.

The first major problem the police faced was the lack of relevant records. During the 40-year interval, considerable destruction of documentation had taken place, most of it by Hitler's Luftwaffe during World War II bombing raids on Swansea. Assize records and police records for the period were now missing. However, a number of people with long memories recalled the case of Mamie Stuart, a dancer who had disappeared in 1919 or 1920. A check on the newspaper records of the time soon turned up a considerable amount of information.

Bigamous marriage

In 1918 a man named George Shotton went through a form of marriage at South Shields with a 26-year-old dancer from Sunderland, Mamie Stuart. Shotton was a marine engineer and travelled widely around the ports supervising ships. He first met Mamie in 1917 when he spent the night with her in Sunderland. George already had a wife and child living in Penarth near Cardiff, but apparently managed to keep two households going.

George and Mamie lived at various addresses in Bristol and South Wales, finally settling in a villa called Ty-Llanwydd in Swansea in November 1919.

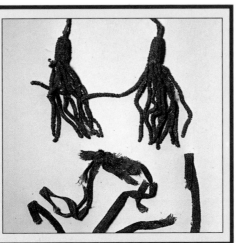

Above and right: Other items included a brass arm chain, some tassels from a dress and a hair clip – still holding brown medium-length hair.

A week later, on 12 November, Mamie sent a lettercard to her parents, Captain and Mrs Stuart. Dutifully, they replied, but their letter was returned marked 'House Closed'. Convinced that there must have been some mistake, Captain Stuart sent a reply-paid telegram to Ty-Llanwydd. This, too, was returned by the post office. Despite their unease, the Stuarts let the matter drop. A few days before Christmas a telegram arrived, apparently from their daughter, wishing the Stuarts "compliments of the season". It was the last they ever heard of her.

In March 1920, the Swansea police were called by the manager of the Grosvenor Hotel to take charge of a large suitcase which had been left by a guest and had lain unclaimed for several months. Further examination showed the case to contain another, rather battered piece of luggage. This in turn revealed two dresses and a pair of shoes, inexplicably cut to shreds; intact were a Bible, a manicure set and some jewellery. At the bottom of the case was a scrap of paper bearing the Sunderland address of Captain and Mrs Stuart, who subsequently identified the remnants as having been clothes belonging to their daughter.

Sinister discovery

At the same time another, more sinister discovery was being made. Behind the washstand in a bedroom of Ty-Llanwydd, a cleaning woman preparing the house for new tenants had found a mildewed brown leather handbag. It contained a few pounds in loose change, and a ration card issued to Mamie Stuart.

At this stage Chief Inspector William Draper was seconded from Scotland Yard to assist the local detectives in their investigation of what was beginning to look increasingly like a case of murder.

Draper's first move was to establish the whereabouts of George Shotton, the elusive husband. In the event, they did not have to look far – Shotton was living in an isolated house in Caswell Bay, named Grey Holme; it was barely two miles from Ty-Llanwydd. With him were his real wife and their small child.

The 'husband's' story

Shotton's story was simple. Yes, he had lived with Mamie Stuart; no, he hadn't married her; and no, he didn't know where she was now. They had quarrelled in early December, parted company and gone their separate ways – he back to his wife, she to heaven knows where.

But the investigating officers were beginning to learn a lot more. For a start, people close to him began to recall incidents from the past, events that showed the ostensibly mild George Shotton to be capable of intense jealousy and violence.

But while there was no excuse for violence, George Shotton had every reason to be jealous. His 'wife' had, indeed, been seeking and distributing favours outside of her relationship with George.

Fearing the worst, the police decided to hedge their bets; a description of Mamie Stuart was circulated throughout Britain, and at the same time they made an exhaustive search of Ty-Llanwydd, dug over

---

Body of evidence

The body in the cave was completely skeletonised, with no flesh to give clues as to who it was. However, the bones themselves were quite informative, and pathologists were able to estimate the age and sex of the victim at the time of death. They also provided a graphic picture of how the killer disposed of the body.

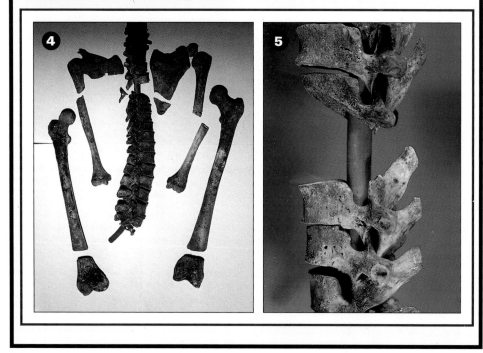

1 The skull from the cave was identified as that of a female. Recently fused bones in the cranium indicated that she had been at most 28 years old when she died.

2 Comparison of the pelvis and hip joint with similar examples confirmed that the victim had been a woman.

3 The dismemberment had not been a clean affair: the numerous partial cuts of bone showed that the killer had obviously had difficulty cutting up the body.

4 It was obvious from the bones that the body had been cut into three equal parts: one cut had been made just above the knees and the other through the middle of the upper arms.

5 The killer had sawn through both shoulder blades. The ribs were not found, but the spine was complete and had been severed level with the arm cuts.

Stormy relationship

Mamie Stuart came from a respectable Sunderland family, but for several years she had been following the somewhat risqué life of a dancer and chorus girl. Mamie met George in South Shields in 1917 and they married – bigamously in his case. After living in Bristol for a time, they took rooms in Swansea in February 1919. In November they rented a villa known as Ty-Llanwydd – 'The Abode of Peace'.

Living in fear

George Shotton was a pleasant-looking man, with considerable powers to charm, but he was also violently jealous. Their landlady in Swansea remembered Mamie saying that George "was not all there", and in a letter to her parents she said: "I don't think I will live with him long. I am very much afraid of him. My life is not worth living."

Cause for jealousy

George had some cause for jealousy: at that time 'theatricals' had an unsavoury reputation, and there is evidence that Mamie lived up to her billing, taking numerous lovers. Was it jealousy which led to Mamie's death?

Mamie Stuart (right) had given up a life in the music halls to 'marry' marine engineer George Shotton. They lived in a number of places around Bristol and South Wales, before settling during 1919 in the prosperous port of Swansea.

Mamie spent several years dancing and singing in concert parties and on variety bills in theatres around Britain.

every inch of its grounds, and combed the countryside around for indications of foul play. The description read:

"Mamie Stuart: age 26; very attractive appearance; height five feet three or four inches: well-built; profusion of dark brown hair, worn bobbed; dark grey eyes; four faint teeth marks on right cheek, the result of a dog bite when a child." But still there was no trace of the missing chorus girl.

Arrested for bigamy

On 29 May 1920, George Shotton was arrested on a charge of bigamy. At Glamorgan Assizes he used the preposterous defence that it was not he, but somebody impersonating him, who had married Mamie Stuart. Shotton then went on and offered an explanation of the suitcase affair. Going back to Ty-Llanwydd after their separation the previous December, he claimed he found a number of Mamie's belongings scattered about, which he collected up, put into a case and dumped during a stay at the Grosvenor Hotel. His bigamy earned George Shotton 18 months' hard labour.

At his trial at Glamorgan Assizes the prosecuting Counsel, Sir Ellis Griffiths

KC, accused him of doing away with Mamie Stuart, but in the absence of a body nothing could be proved.

Over the ensuing years, the mystery was regularly revived by newspapers. Then, in 1950, a dentist bought the house at Caswell Bay and, during drainage work, discovered a pit against the back of the house, near a hole in the foundations through to the space beneath the floorboards of the dining room. The pit had been filled with quicklime, but all that was found in it was one lady's shoe.

Eventually, in 1961 the skeleton was found by the pot-holers in the lead mine at Brandy Cove.

Was this Mamie?

The height corresponded to that of Mamie Stuart: the age range of 23-28 fitted her age of 26 at the time of her disappearance; and the hair in the celluloid slide was similar to her brown hair colour. The brass chain found with the body matched up with an arm chain that Mamie's sister had reported the missing woman had habitually worn.

The only photograph of Mamie Stuart was that contained in old newspaper files

from 1920, when her disappearance and the bigamy trial were in the news. The police used this photograph to make a 'photo-fit' by superimposing a transparency copy over a photograph of the skull in the same orientation and degree of enlargement. The degree of correspondence was excellent, and although it was not claimed to be a positive identification, there was certainly no evidence of a discrepancy between the two.

Cause of death

No dental records were available for Mamie Stuart, though general information suggested that she had a false front tooth. However, several teeth were missing from the skull, presumably due to post-mortem loss, and were not recovered from the cave.

Dr Lester James told the coroner that he could not offer any cause of death, as no organs or soft tissues were present. He excluded any head injury, but said that strangulation, stabbing or even a gunshot could have killed Mamie, as long as they left no mark of damage on the bones.

An inquest was held at Gowerton on 14 December 1961. The proceedings were

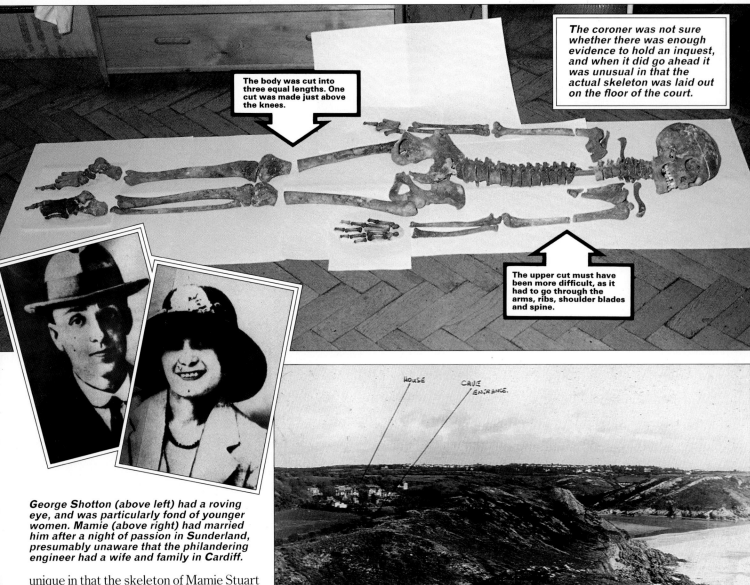

The body was cut into three equal lengths. One cut was made just above the knees.

The coroner was not sure whether there was enough evidence to hold an inquest, and when it did go ahead it was unusual in that the actual skeleton was laid out on the floor of the court.

The upper cut must have been more difficult, as it had to go through the arms, ribs, shoulder blades and spine.

HOUSE   CAVE ENTRANCE.

George Shotton (above left) had a roving eye, and was particularly fond of younger women. Mamie (above right) had married him after a night of passion in Sunderland, presumably unaware that the philandering engineer had a wife and family in Cardiff.

unique in that the skeleton of Mamie Stuart was laid out on a table in the well of the court, reminiscent of the medieval inquests when the coroner and jury assembled around the body.

Postman's encounter

One witness was a retired 83-year-old postman from Mumbles, Swansea, who had delivered mail to both houses in which Mamie Stuart and George Shotton lived. He remembered one occasion when a small yellow van was parked outside Shotton's front gate. Shotton struggled out with a bulky sack, which he put in the back of the van. When the postman offered to help, Shotton cried: "No, no, no! Oh God, you gave me a fright, I thought it was a policeman!"

Pieces of rotted sacking were found in the cave with the skeleton, and it was suggested that the postman's encounter had been at the actual moment when the three parts of the body were being transported to the old mine.

The police then investigated the movements of George Shotton after he finished his 18-month prison sentence for bigamy in the early 1920s. He was traced to Tintern,

Mamie and George lived in a detached villa on Caswell Bay, a beauty spot about six miles from Swansea. Mamie's clandestine grave was a mere 200 yards from the house.

but some years later a newspaper had revived the story and he promptly left. Shotton appeared to be living in London until 1938, when he was once more in trouble, being sent to prison again for 12 months for holding up his sister with a revolver at Fareham near Portsmouth. Following this he turned up in Bristol, working for an aircraft company and lodging at various places in the Fishponds area.

When the police went looking for Shotton after the discovery of the skeleton, they found him – in Bristol's Arnos Vale Cemetery, having died of natural causes in April 1958 at the age of 78.

At the conclusion of the inquest (which the coroner held after consultation with the Home Office, as he was not sure if the remains constituted sufficient for an inquest),

a verdict of murder was returned, naming George Shotton as the killer. Changes in coroners' legislation would now make this impossible, but in 1961 a coroner's jury still had the power to bring in a verdict of murder and name the culprit.

Coroner's quote

Unusually for the sombre business of an inquest – though perhaps not so unusual in bardic Wales – the coroner, Mr D. R. James, publicly quoted a remarkably appropriate passage from a poem from Swinburn: "Between highland and lowland, by the coin of the cliff by the silver sea, without a grave, uncoffined, unknelled and unknown"!

This extraordinary story of a 40-year-old homicide, where the perpetrator lay peacefully in his grave when the police caught up with him, is probably unique in the annals of British crime. □